MODEL RAILWAYS

A Complete Guide to the Hobby

DAVE LOWERY

ARGUS BOOKS

Argus Books
Argus House
Boundary Way
Hemel Hempstead
Herts HP2 7ST
England

First published by Argus Books 1992

ISBN 1 85486 074 7

Phototypesetting by Photoprint
Printed and bound in Great Britain by
William Clowes Ltd. Beccles.

MODEL RAILWAYS

CONTENTS

Acknowledgements		8
Foreword		9
Chapter 1	What to Model?	11
Chapter 2	What's Available?	17
Chapter 3	Scale and Gauges	21
Chapter 4	Ready-to-Run Locos in OO/HO	29
Chapter 5	Planning a Layout	35
Chapter 6	Why a Baseboard?	41
Chapter 7	Diorama or Layout?	45
Chapter 8	Construction	49
Chapter 9	Permanent Way	57
Chapter 10	Wiring Up	61
Chapter 11	Electrics Explained	65
Chapter 12	'Digital' Computer Control	71
Chapter 13	Scenics	75
Chapter 14	Trees	81
Chapter 15	Buildings	89
Chapter 16	Hints and Tips	97
Chapter 17	Tools	101
Chapter 18	Stock	107
Chapter 19	White Metal Kits	111
Chapter 20	Building 'O' Gauge 'Electrics'	115
Chapter 21	Painting and Lining	123
Chapter 22	Starting from Scratch	135
Appendix A	UK Manufacturers and Suppliers	141
Appendix B	Glossary	143

DEDICATION

To Samantha for just being herself.

ACKNOWLEDGEMENTS

My thanks go to Hornby Railways, in particular Simon Kohlor. To Ken Court of Riko International, who import the excellent Lima range of locos and stock. To Tony Osborn, proprietor of Model Images, Stewart Hine for explaining the electrics, Steve Barnfield for his notes on painting and lining, Eric Kemp for his tree-making and Peter Holland for the drawings. Also to various authors who contributed to the 'special' publications *Starting Model Railways*, and *Building Model Railway Kits*.

FOREWORD

Argus Specialist Publications, through *Model Railways* magazine, have, over the years, produced a number of one-off 'specials' dealing with every conceivable aspect of the model railway world. It is from these publications that I have drawn inspiration and ideas for this 'complete guide', which is packed full of ideas and information on all aspects of the hobby.

I have concentrated on the more colourful aspects of model railways and I hope you enjoy the craftsmanship shown here by the many talented modellers I've brought together for you.

CHAPTER 1
WHAT TO MODEL?

There are nearly as many kinds of model railways as there are railway modellers, so, before deciding what to model, think about what you want from the hobby. Is your chief interest operation, scenery, or loco building? Do you prefer the mainline, branchline or light-railway scene, the activity of a station or the occasionally broken piece of a line between stations? Or do you simply need a test-track where your latest loco can be put through its paces? The main line scene requires either a smaller scale or more obvious compression of the length of trains and the size of stations: if your preference is for this type of railway, are you prepared for the extra space, extra work or compromises that this will involve?

Any model railway that is more than just a test-track needs a convincing and coherent 'story' behind it. This means that the builder must have thought about where the line is supposed to be situated, why it was built (for example to carry coal from mines to a seaport or to bring farm produce into a developing township) and what period is illustrated by the model. There is an immense scope for ideas in the area of layout planning. You can model a line which actually exists, or has existed, finding out from published histories or local records how the place looked in the chosen period; you can place an imaginary line, either independent or owned by one of the 'Big Four', in a real location, but make sure there is a real reason for the railway being there; or you can model part of a real company in an imaginary location – some very fine layouts have been built by modellers who invented not only the railway but also the town and even the entire country in which it was located!

The important thing is that the railway should be consistent within itself and with its surroundings. If you think this all too pedantic, it is only necessary to visit a few model railway exhibitions and look at the different types of layouts on show; those

Fabia, aged 7 and Carla, aged 4 enjoying a small starter 'Thomas the Tank Engine' train set.

Modern image may
appeal to you. A Lima
Deltic pulling a rake of
Mk 1 coaches passes a
freight yard.

Going back several years
to the early diesels. Ian
Futers, an established
modeller, stands by one of
his loves.

that really 'come across' and involve the spectator are those where all the above questions have been fully considered.

The Prototype

Also to be considered in choosing a theme is the prototype – the original 12in to the foot from which model railways originate. The setting for the layout can be based on a real location or it can be totally imaginary; it can be set in this country or abroad; or it can be built to portray any particular historical period (bearing in mind that it would look a bit odd if you were to see an InterCity 125 roaring past a background of the Battle of Hastings!). This is where your imagination can really be let loose. Many modellers approach this in the same way as a painter creating a scheme on canvas – but in this medium it is three-dimensional. Remember, once you begin to scenic a layout, you're no longer 'playing with a train set', you're building a model railway.

The next step is to decide upon a region. Nowadays, the main railway grid is run by British Rail, although there are also various tourist railways, industrial railways and a few metropolitan lines. The history of the railway in Britain is long and complex and would fill a fair-sized bookshelf, but a basic understanding will help in your choice of region.

Up until 1923, there were over a hundred independently owned railways throughout Britain. In 1923, Parliament engineered a reorganisation, merging all of them into four large companies known as the 'Big Four'. These were the London Midland and Scottish Railway (LMS or LMSR), the London and North Eastern Railway (LNER), the Great Western Railway (GWR) and the Southern Railway (SR). In 1948 they were nationalised and came under the banner of British Railways, evolving in 1964 into British Rail. Out of the original 'Big Four', only the

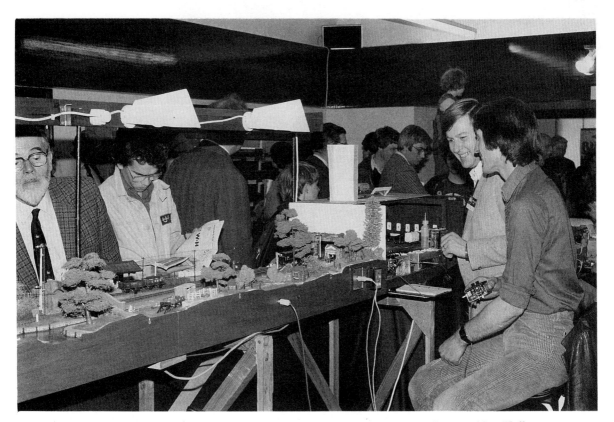

One of my layouts at an exhibition, another area of enjoyment, along with colleague Alan Hall.

A snow scene is different and uses a lot of commercial products, mainly from Europe.

Not all layouts have to be full of trains. This high street is built from resin moulded kits.

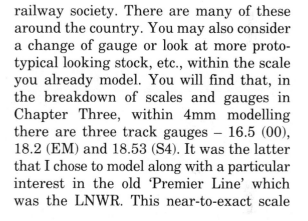

This Fleischmann exhibition layout visits most of the major shows. This one is in the smaller N-gauge scale.

GWR managed to retain its own identity, in that most of its stock remained very much the same after the amalgamation. Individual and distinctive liveries stayed the same and it is mainly for this reason that more GWR models are available from the trade.

Model Railway Societies

Having chosen a theme and a region, you might like to think about joining a model railway society. There are many of these around the country. You may also consider a change of gauge or look at more proto-typical looking stock, etc., within the scale you already model. You will find that, in the breakdown of scales and gauges in Chapter Three, within 4mm modelling there are three track gauges – 16.5 (00), 18.2 (EM) and 18.53 (S4). It was the latter that I chose to model along with a particular interest in the old 'Premier Line' which was the LNWR. This near-to-exact scale

Striving for realism, both in the railway and environment. One of my layouts.

The steam period – the location here being North Wales – will always appeal.

modelling satisfied my needs and I include, throughout the book, photos of my two exhibition layouts 'Bevleys' and 'Bevet' that have attended over 50 exhibitions up and down the country.

Become a member of a club where experience, advice and encouragement will usually be showered upon you and you can gain the opportunity to exhibit your work . . . go on, have a go.

CHAPTER 2
WHAT'S AVAILABLE?

Before planning your layout, or deciding on the region or area of the hobby that most appeals, take a look around your local model shop. When you see the range of sets, accessories, stock and scenic materials available, you should easily come to a decision. A particular model of a loco or train, or even a kit of parts for building, may appeal to you and point the way for future model railway projects.

By far the most popular gauge is OO/HO and here the market leader is Hornby Hobbies. Produced in a factory in Margate, Kent, this manufacturer has been trading for many years under a variety of name changes. Some of these include Tri-ang, Tri-ang/Hornby, Hornby/Triang and, currently Hornby Railways. Other manufacturers producing British outline railways are Lima, manufactured in Italy, Dapol, Replica and Bachmann. For the European modeller, both Marklin and Fleischmann are easily available but not in the same volume as the British companies.

For N-gauge, the biggest manufacturer of British outline is Graham Farish, based at Poole in Dorset. The range covers both steam and diesel outline and now even includes the new East Coast mainline InterCity 225 overhead electric trains. This is made up of the class 91 electric loco, Mk 4 plug door coaches and BR Mk 4 (DVT). Locos, coaches and rolling stock are available for the various periods, and they really are superb models. Minitrix also

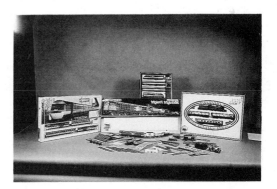

Lima, Dapol and Hornby sets are shown here with the Hornby Railways' Midnight Freight displayed.

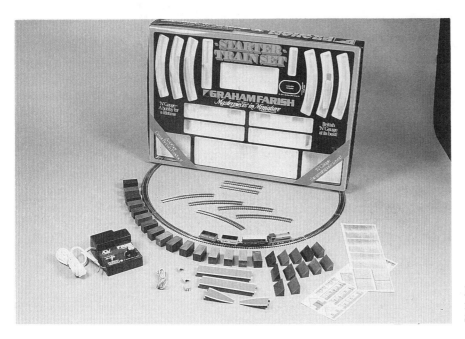

For the N-gauge modeller, a Starter Train Set from Graham Farish.

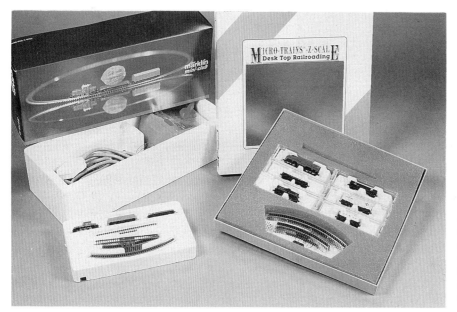

Although not of British origin but still of interest are these Z-gauge sets (the smallest commerically produced) available from Marklin and the US Micro-Trains.

produce British outline which is imported into this country and, for the European modeller, Marklin and Fleischmann again market excellent products including track-work.

'O' gauge tends to be more a case of building your own stock from ranges of kits from numerous manufacturers. Lima, however, produce a limited range of ready-to-run stock in a number of different liveries.

Most of these manufacturers have available catalogues which give complete details of all sets, ranging from the basic starter to the deluxe, and these can form an ideal basis for your project. Also included in the catalogues are all the other stock items, locos, accessories and spares. You

Two other sources of useful information are also by me, *Build a Model Railway* – Argus Books and *How to Build a Model Railway* – Chess Valley Videos.

will most certainly need some extras to add to your basic set, and there is a multitude of publications to help you get started. Here are a few you may find useful:

Build a Model Railway Layout, Dave Lowery, Argus Books.
Complete plan and step-by-step instructions for a OO/HO layout.
How to Build a Model Railway Video, Dave Lowery, Chess Valley.
Complete step-by-step guide to building an N-gauge layout.
OO Gauge Track Plans 6th edition, Hornby Railways.

PSL Book of Model Railway Track Plans, C J Freezer, Patrick Stephens.

To complement the basic trains, there is a wide range of accessories that can enhance your model railway and bring it to life. You may want to feature the countryside, so trees, hedges, fences and farm-type buildings are required, while a city-style model requires retaining walls, warehouses, large station buildings etc. All of these, and more, are available from many sources and various manufacturers. Where possible, always go to a recognised model shop where you'll get sound, helpful advice and after-sales service.

CHAPTER 3
SCALE AND GAUGES

The selection of the most suitable gauge and scale for a model railway is always a compromise between conflicting factors. As one of the first and most important decisions to be made when planning a layout, it needs careful thought.

First of all, it is necessary to understand clearly the terms 'gauge' and 'scale', which are often confused. *Gauge* is the distance between the inside faces of the running rails; *scale* is the factor relating dimension on the prototype to its equivalent on the model. Of course, the gauge is itself a prototype dimension – at least to begin with – and so the two are related, but not as directly as one may assume.

The 'standard gauge' of 4ft 8½in (1435mm) began as an attempt to standardise the gauges of a host of existing colliery tramways, hence the very unround figure. This gauge spread all over the world, but is by no means universal. Brunel's 7ft gauge for the original Great Western Railway is well known; Ireland, Spain and India use gauges in excess of 5ft; while, at the other end of the scale, the Ffestiniog and Vale of Rheifol railways carry heavy tourist traffic on a gauge of 1ft 11½in.

Even so, it is not simply a matter of using the scale to convert the prototype gauge to that of the model – or, as more often happens, of finding out to what scale the model should be built to fit an existing standard model railway gauge. A railway is a very large item compared with the rooms into which our models have to fit; therefore, almost all model railways have to operate round sharper curves and up steeper gradients than their full-size counterparts. Commercial models, designed primarily as toys, have to be able to run reasonably, despite unevenly-assembled track, and to be handled by unskilled young fingers. For these reasons, most models have wider wheel treads and deeper and thicker flanges than they would in exact scale and, as the width over

Comparison of sizes is shown clearly with these three coaches. At the back, 'O' gauge; centre, OO/HO; and in the front N-gauge.

A Micro-Trains F7
Z-gauge from the USA.

the outer faces of the wheels is limited, the gauge is commonly reduced to keep it within a near-scale limit. Add to this a series of well-intended but doomed efforts to 'rationalise' scales to make both gauge and scale come out to some sort of round figure, and you can see why the gauge of small railway models is hardly ever the exact scale equivalent. Often there are several different gauges for a single scale, or vice versa.

As I mentioned previously, railway equipment is very big – even in N, one of the smallest common scales, a typical express train can be over 5ft long, and a station to accommodate it with approach roads may come out to twice that length. Thus the modeller who favours mainline practice, and has limited space, will want to opt for the smallest practicable scale. On the other hand, scratchbuilding and kit assembly in very small scales – though by no means as impossible as is often claimed – requires patience and skill, and, if the layout is to be handled by children, they may find difficulty in re-railing and coupling very small vehicles. Large-scale models take longer to make due to the

N-gauge interest is well satisfied in this country by Graham Farish with their excellent 2–6–4 Tank.

sheer size of the parts and the greater amount of detail that is needed to make a convincing replica; and the 'ground rent' and material cost of even a scratchbuilt Gauge 1 layout are not to be taken lightly. On the other hand, the sharper the curves (in proportion to the scale) the more difficult it will be to get good running. Even commercial models designed to run round a 15in radius perform better and look more realistic on gentler curves; the rule of thumb of 'one foot radius per mile per foot scale' is a good recipe for trouble-free operation and, incidentally, corresponds very closely with BR's minimum-curve requirement. The sharpness of curves is also governed by the type of stock modelled – small 4- and 6-wheeled locos and coaches can tolerate much sharper curves than long bogie coaches and express locos – and by whether the modeller finds acceptable or not the appearance of 'coarse scale' wheels (in which the exaggeration of tread and flange dimensions is greater).

Smaller Gauges

It is often stated that a narrow-gauge prototype saves space. While it is true that narrow-gauge stock can negotiate much tighter curves than their standard-gauge counterparts – indeed, this was the reason for the adoption of narrow gauge in most full-size lines – the scale is what governs the overall size of the layout. It is difficult to believe in model travellers waiting half-an-hour for a train to make a journey which they could obviously walk in five minutes! A final, practical factor affecting the choice of scale is the amount of ready-to-run and kit equipment available, and the amount of adaptation or scratchbuilding which the individual modeller is prepared to do.

In the following summary of the principal modelling scales and gauges, I have assumed a standard-gauge prototype, except at the end. You will notice that there is a switch between 'Gauge O' and

I built this Gem 2–4–2T of the LNWR to P4, 18.83 gauge. The flanges and track are exact scale.

'S Gauge' – this is in accordance with the usual practice. It will also be seen that many of the scales are on the basis of so many millimetres per foot; this is a result of trying to make a 4ft 8½in come out to a round figure in any system of units, and is not as crazy as it sounds in a country where nearly all the prototypes are increasingly becoming metric. In any case, the modeller will quickly become 'bilingual' and many of the conversions between the two systems can be approximated mentally.

The various popular gauges in actual size from Gauge 1 to Z-gauge.

Gauge 1

Gauge 1 was once considered the smallest practical gauge for a model railway but is now nearly the biggest. The gauge is 1¾in (44.45mm) and the scale most commonly used is 10mm/ft; some modellers prefer ⅜in/ft (1/32) which gives a more accurate gauge/scale ratio and makes scaling from

prototype drawings easier. Most Gauge 1 layouts are out-of-doors and require a larger-than-average garden; ready-to-run models are very expensive and even the materials for scratchbuilding cost quite a lot due to the sheer size. The advantages of the large scale lie in the closeness of the models' behaviour to the prototype; their mass gives realistic coasting and a feeling of 'real railway' operation. It is the smallest scale in which reliable live-steam locos can be built without exceptional skill or facilities.

Gauge 'O'

Gauge 'O' is 32mm between the rails and the usual scale is 7mm/ft. The scale shares the advantages of Gauge 1 to a limited extent but can be accommodated in small gardens or large lofts. Not much ready-made equipment is available but the range of kits and parts is quite good.

S Gauge

S Gauge uses a scale of 3/16in/ft (1/64) and a gauge of ⅞in. There is little commercial support but the S Gauge Society provides a range of essential supplies.

HO Gauge

HO Gauge is literary 'Half O' with a gauge of 16.5mm and a scale of 3.5mm/ft. It is standard on the Continent and in America, but is seldom used for models of British prototype. The British counterpart is OO Gauge.

OO Gauge

OO Gauge is, again, 16.5mm between rails but, due to the early problems in making motors small enough to fit into the restricted British loading gauge, a compromise scale of 4mm/ft was adopted.

Lima class 47 in grey Civils livery and class 31 in Mainline livery. Both are OO/HO gauge.

This is the most widely-used scale/gauge combination in the UK and an enormous range of ready-to-run models and kits is available.

EM and Scalefour

EM Gauge and Protofour/Scalefour represent attempts to improve the scale/gauge ratio while taking advantage of the otherwise excellent models and kits at the upper end of the OO gauge market. EM is 18.2mm between rails; S4 and P4, with a gauge of 18.83mm, have proved that reliable running can be obtained with almost exact-scale wheel standards, given reasonable care. The relevant societies provide the necessary parts for conversion and there is some support from the commercial kit market.

TT Gauge

TT Gauge (standing for 'Table Top') originated in the USA with a track gauge of 12mm and a scale of 1/120, giving an excellent scale/gauge ratio and allowing a layout in less space than HO. British TT was introduced by Triang to 3mm/ft scale; it proved a commercial failure but the scale of 3mm/ft (or ¼mm:1in) proved excellent for the British modeller, and there is a flourishing 3mm Society and a

buoyant market in secondhand Triang TT items which enable a modeller with some building ability to produce layouts in this scale with few problems. Predictably, 13.5mm and 14.2mm gauge standards have appeared, corresponding to EM and P4.

N-Gauge

N-Gauge – currently the most popular size after OO – has a track gauge of 9mm (the word for 'nine' in nearly all European languages begins with N) and a scale of 1/160 for Continental and American models. Once again, British N is different, having a scale of 1/148 or 21/16mm/ft. Prices are much the same as for OO items and the range is nearly as wide, but there is a shortage of accurate steam loco models.

2mm Scale

2mm Scale with a track gauge of 9.5mm was first used some 50 years ago, by a few experimental modellers. During the Second World War, interest in the scale grew, due to the shortage of modelling materials, and the track gauge has since been refined to the exact scale figure of 9.42mm. The 2mm Scale Association pro-

A kit-built 08 shunter shows how near the real thing you can get with models in the larger 'O' gauge, also from my collection.

vides a good range of essential parts, and some commercial N-gauge items and kits can be adapted – some kits are actually made to 2mm size.

Z-Gauge

Z-Gauge is the latest and smallest to appear on the scene. At present, only Marklin and Kadee produce equipment for this very small scale with a track gauge of 6.5mm and a scale of 1/220. Prices are higher than for the equivalent N-gauge items.

Narrow Gauge

The variety of scale/gauge combinations for narrow-gauge modelling is quite bewildering. The general principle is to use the scenic accessories and some rolling-stock parts from one scale with track and locomotive mechanisms from a smaller one. A few examples are:

1/24 scale on G1 track representing metre gauge (LGB)
16mm/ft scale on GO track representing 2ft gauge

4mm scale on TT track representing 3ft or metre gauge
4mm scale on N track representing 2ft 3in gauge
2mm or N on Z track representing metre gauge.

Common Name	Scale	Gauge	Ratio
Gauge 1	10mm/ft	44.45mm	1/32
'O' Gauge	7mm/ft	32mm	1/43
*OO	4mm/ft	16.5mm	1/76
*HO	3.5mm/ft	16.5mm	1/87
TT	3mm/ft	12mm	1/120
N	2mm/ft	9mm	1/160 European or 1/148 British
Z	–	6.5mm	1/220

* Note, because of the common track gauge (16.5mm), these two are bracketed together, thus we have OO/HO.

The table overleaf gives the leading dimensions for each of the scale/gauge combinations commonly used in the UK. As far as possible, the figures are those recommended by the BRMSB. The dimension B in the diagram overleaf should be adhered to as closely as possible. No official figures for Z gauge are available, and the figures given are based on measurements of Marklin equipment.

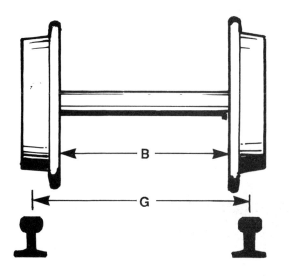

	Scale	G		B	
	in	in	mm	in	mm
1	10mm/ft	1¾	44.45	1.574	40.0
1	⅜ub/ft	1¾	44.45	1.574	40.0
1F	10mm/ft	1.771	45.0	1.654	42.0
'0'	7mm/ft	1.259	32.0	1.102	28.0
0F	7mm/ft	1.259	32.0	1.141	29.0
S	3/16/ft	0.875	22.23	.781	19.85
S4/P4	4mm/ft	0.741	18.83	.703	17.87
EM	4mm/ft	0.709	18.0	.649	16.5
OO/HO	4mm/ft 3.5/ft	0.649	16.5	.570	14.5
TT	3mm/ft	0.472	12.0	.406	10.31
N	1/160 1/148	0.354	9.0	.291	7.4
2mm	2mm/ft	0.371	9.42	.336	8.5
Z	1/220	0.256	6.5	.216	5.5

B– back-to-back measurement between the inside of the pair of wheels. G– track gauge is the distance between the centre of each rail.

CHAPTER 4
READY-TO-RUN LOCOS IN OO/HO

Hornby Railways' class 91 electric loco (top) and (bottom) class 86 electric loco.

The following listing is a taster of just what is available to you from the various major manufacturers in the more popular OO/HO gauge. This list covers steam, diesel and electric motive power that run on the Standard (4ft 8½in.) gauge prototype.

Much of the information contained herein has been taken from each supplier's individual list or catalogue. The ready-to-run prices are approximate and prices for the same basic model can vary according to the amount of finishing work involved in the particular version purchased. The extreme example of this must be the Dapol 'Terrier', where you can pay from £34.50 for the basic model, and up to £60 for the same loco offered in a limited edition finish. Also, I am aware that there are more ready-to-run models available in most model shops than listed here, some models still being on the shelves although not offered in current catalogues. The prices shown are approximate and can vary according to the particular model chosen.

Lima concentrate on modern traction. Seen here are two locos, a class 33 (top) and class 47 (bottom) both in Civils 'Dutch' livery.

Bachmann 4–6–0 GWR
Manor class.

Dapol have released the
0–6–0 Terrier track in a
number of liveries.

Latest Parcels livery is
reproduced in miniature
by Graham Farish in
these N-gauge models.

GWR Steam

Manufacturer	*Model*		*Price*
Hornby	2721	0–6–0PT	£31
Replica	57XX	0–6–0PT	£27
Lima	94XX	0–6–0PT	£29
Dapol	Dean Goods	0–6–0	£44
Replica	Collett Goods	0–6–0	£30
Dapol	66XX	0–6–2T	£30
Lima	45XX	2–6–2T	£39
Dapol	61XX	2–6–2T	£38
Dapol	43XX	2–6–0	£35
Dapol	County	4–6–0	£52
Bachmann	Manor	4–6–0	£46
Wrenn	Castle	4–6–0	£70
Dapol	Castle	4–6–0	£44
Lima	King	4–6–0	£49
Hornby	King	4–6–0	£52
Dapol	ExLBSC Terrior	0–6–0Tvia WC & P	£35

LMS Steam

Manufacturer	*Model*		*Price*
Dapol	0F	0–4–0ST (L&Y)	£22–£29
Hornby	3F	0–6–0T	£31
Dapol	2P	4–4–0	£44
Dapol	Royal Scot	4–6–0	£35–£41
Wrenn	Royal Scot	4–6–0	£75
Bachmann	Rebuilt Patriot	4–6–0	£51
Dapol	Rebuilt Patriot	4–6–0	£41
Dapol	Jubilee	4–6–0	£41
Bachmann	Jubilee	4–6–0	£51
Hornby	Princess	4–6–2	£62
Wrenn	Coronation/Duchess	4–6–2	£75
Hornby	8F	2–8–0	£62
Wrenn	8F	2–8–0	£75

BR Steam

Manufacturer	*Model*		*Price*
Hornby	9F	2–10–0	£57–£60
Hornby	Britannia	4–6–2	£58
Bachman	Class 4	4–6–0 with choice of BR1B or BR2 tender and single/double chimney	£41
Wrenn	Class 4	2–6–4T	£59
Dapol	Austerity	0–6–0ST	£35

Bachmann 4–6–0 mixed traffic class 4 in BR livery.

One for the 'O' gauge
enthusiasts is this class
33 in triple grey livery
allocated to Construction
sub-sector. Available
from Lima.

Hornby Railways' Stanier 8F 2–8–0.

LNER Steam

Manufacturer	Model	Price
Hornby	A1 4–6–2	£57
Hornby	A4 4–6–2	£62
Wrenn	A4 4–6–2	£77
Replica	B1 4–6–0	£42
Lima	J50 0–6–0T (GNR)	£24
Bachmann	J72 0–6–0T (NER)	£26
Dapol	J94 0–6–0ST (Austerity)	£35
Dapol	N2 0–6–0T (GNR)	£25
Wrenn	N2 0–6–2T (GNR)	£35
Dapol	J94 0–6–0ST (Austerity)	£35

Southern Steam

Manufacturer	Model	Price
Dapol	A1/A1X 0–6–0T (LBSC)	£35–£60
Wrenn	R1 0–6–0T (Rebuilt SER)	£26
Hornby	V (Schools) 4–4–0	£55
Wrenn	Rebuilt WC/BoB 4–6–2 (BR)	£71

Diesel & Electric Locos

Class	Manufacturer	Price
03	Replica	£27
06	Hornby	£20
08/09	Lima	£24–£30
08/09	Hornby	£27
08/09	Wrenn	£35
20	Lima	£25–£33
20	Wrenn	£41
25	Hornby	£25
26	Lima	£28
27	Lima	£28
31	Lima	£30–£37
31	Dapol	£33
33	Lima	£23–£29
37	Lima	£30
37	Hornby	£30
40	Lima	£30–£33
45/46	Lima	£35
45/46	Replica	£27
47	Lima	£26–£35
47	Hornby	£27–£32
50	Lima	£24–£26
55	Lima	£23–£25
56	Dapol	£30
58	Hornby	£36
73	Lima	£28–£30
86	Hornby	£33
87	Lima	£30–£38
90	Hornby	£34
90	Lima (release imminent	
91	Hornby	£34
43xxx HST	Power Cars Lima	£42
43xxx HST	Power Cars Hornby	£47

Note: prices are approximate and will vary – they are intended as a guide only.

CHAPTER 5
PLANNING A LAYOUT

The subtitle for this chapter should be 'don't fall into the old trap'! The biggest single failing of most layout designers is to take a board and then design a layout to fit it. Design your layout first and, once its final design has been accepted, fit the woodwork around it. This way, only minimal changes will be required.

First list the requirements of the layout you want to build – try to think of as many things as possible for your list. Here are some suggestions I have put down for a layout I've used as a good basic example with a degree of scope:

Mainline running – single circuit
Terminus station – with return loop
To accommodate a number of fixed trains – storage sidings
Each train to have two locos – plenty of loco shed space
Main controller and Shunt controller – independent of each other

From these headings, I designed the resulting layout. Now, expanding the main points further, I'll show you the scope of this layout in both the type of stock it can carry and its potential operation. So, starting with the terminus, I decided that a loco and three coaches was a reasonable length train to be accommodated in the platform. Plus there had to be enough room to hold the second engine which brought the train in. The Hornby overall roof is very attractive and, as I mentioned earlier, certain things appeal when deciding on what type of layout to build. This was one thing that I wanted to include.

The main theme is running steam trains from different regions in the late British Railways period. This allows one train to have two locos: for example the *Mallard* with train can also be paired with, say, the *Flying Scotsman*. The requirement to run a number of different trains means that they need to be stored somewhere when not in use. I resolved this by a series of storage sidings under the main terminus on the lower levels. This two level layout allows the building of embankments etc., up to the terminus.

Sharp Curves

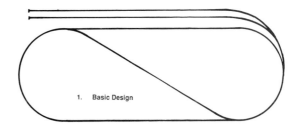

Simple circuit with reverse curve and terminus.

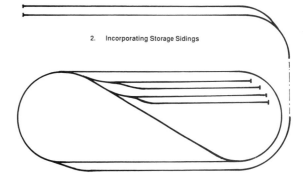

Storage sidings need to be at a lower level with the terminus at a higher level.

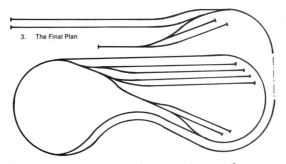

This gives storage, mainline running, stock movements, terminus, loco sheds, banker and goods movements.

Under the roof on a
finished layout is the
accommodation for a loco
and three coaches.

The loco shed on the
upper level holds three
engines ready to couple-
up to trains in the main
terminus.

One of the worst properties of train sets
are the sharp radius curves – a necessary
evil, otherwise layouts would need 4ft
minimum curves which would make them
too big. This needs to be very seriously
considered when entering 'fine scale' modelling. So, somehow, these end curves will
have to be disguised just leaving the
straight centre section showing.

Something not required, but usually

present on a steam layout, is a turntable.
Because we have a reverse curve, this
accessory is not necessary as, when the
loco is run through the reverse loop, it will,
in fact, be facing the other way. A turntable also takes up quite a lot of room and
is fairly expensive; it is the sort of thing
that can be added at a later date. You
should, therefore, allow room to accommodate this and include it on the basic plan,

The lower level sidings are for a goods train at the back and a loco spur at the front. The latter will also hold a 'banker', a loco that will help another train up the embankment.

indicated in dotted lines, perhaps, as a later development. Because of the abundance of locos to be accommodated for the trains, two loco areas are required, one on the lower level as a holding siding into

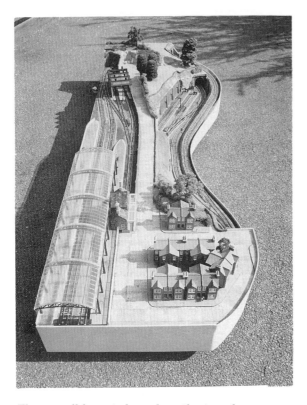

The overall layout shows how the two sharp curves at the ends of the layout are hidden. One under a town scene, the other under a hill.

which locos are put once they've been turned using the reverse loop. They then wait until they can go 'light engine' back up to the main shed.

To hide the sharp curves at the ends, I decided to create some sort of town at the terminus station end. Here the excellent Victorian shops and houses (again from Hornby) can be used. At the other end, some sort of mountain or hill will cover the two tracks; that will be a case of trial and error once the tracks have been laid.

Planning Stage

As you can see, the planning stage of any layout project is very important and a great deal of care has to be taken. As I mentioned earlier, try to include as much as you can on the plan, even down to the routes the wires will take for the electric points, where the controller goes, and where the switches and point levers are situated.

Finally, always try to leave access points to the main track circuits so that the layout can be extended at a later stage. While on this subject, the space available will govern the area the layout can occupy. Don't get carried away by trying to produce Euston or Paddington as your first

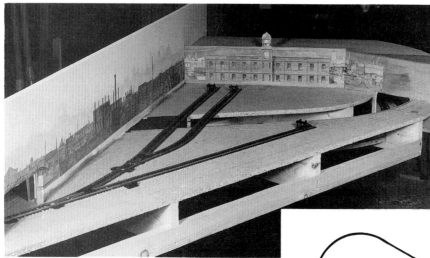

On the other side of the central backscene will be the city terminus. The underpass can be seen in this view.

layout; start small to gain experience and then expand just like the real thing did in its formative years. I will show you that a good layout, when finished off with proper drapes and ply edging, can be a prominent feature in a room – in fact a positive focal point. To show an alternative method of construction using 4in × 1in cross pieces

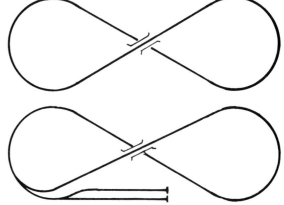

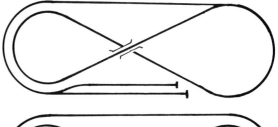

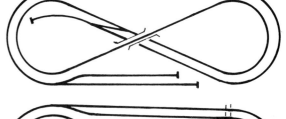

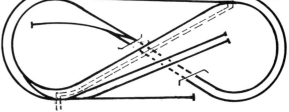

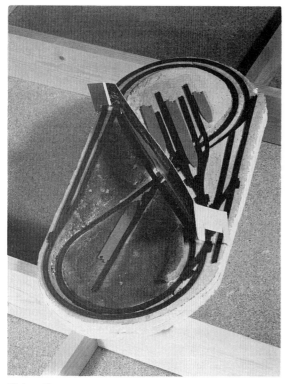

Using the components, a small-scale replica of your proposed layout can be made up to make sure of its practicalities.

How the design of a typical layout goes through its progressive stages, until it reaches its final form. From a simple figure of eight it now has a terminus, branchline, mainline and two distinct scenes.

instead of 2in × 1in, I've included another variation on the basic design. This time, the running line drops down and the terminus stays level. But, by using a back- scene across its centre, it will give two different scenes. I will point out the varia- tions in construction during construction of both projects.

CHAPTER 6
WHY A BASEBOARD?

The single most important necessity for model railway locomotives and stock is to keep them clean, well maintained and, particularly, free from fluff. It never ceases to amaze me just how fluff manages to accumulate into engine mechanisms. This causes clogging of the wheels, gears and axles and removes the oil which is so important for smooth running. So how do we get round this? The solution is to make a permanent base or baseboard, usually consisting of a softwood framework with a suitable covering. This can be ply, chipboard or Sundeala. This last covering is available from most specialist model railway shops and is an ideal surface. Its advantage over, say, chipboard is that it is lighter, but will require more cross-braces of softwood than chipboard since it will sag over a longer length. This will result in undulating trackwork, which we do not want.

As well as keeping the layout free from dirt, a firm base allows easy transport once the trackwork is fixed, so it can easily be stored or taken to other venues, for example an exhibition. Storage is all-important. Because of their nature, model

Once legs have been added, the baseboard becomes free-standing and is much easier to work on.

railways tend to take up a large amount of space. So, once you have finished with it after an operating session (a term used by the bigger kids among us – really we're all just playing), you can store it so that normal household life can resume. Storage can be under a bed (ideal on a baseboard

This set-up should be avoided at all costs. Do not lay a train set out on the lounge carpet – it will cause no end of problems.

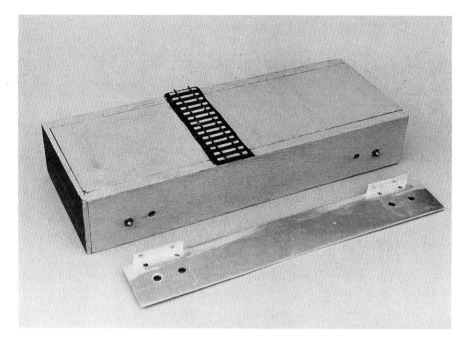

A simple baseboard can be constructed from a 2in × 1in softwood framework. To line up several boards, a dowelling jig can be used.

A completely new form of baseboard construction was introduced by the Model Railway Club using ply and softwood to form strong beams.

The Manchester MRC used a lot of ply formers for their extensive layout and reduced the weight by removing unwanted sections without loss of strength.

For multiple track levels, uprights can be put in to hold up sub-bases.

fitted with castors), folded up against a wall or, as I once saw in a house, actually slung from the ceiling by pulleys and ropes, pulled up out of the way when not in use – most ingenious!

The design I have chosen allows the baseboard to be free-standing, with its own legs that will fold up underneath when not is use, and the layout can be stored on its side against a wall. A simple system of folding cross-stays on the legs allows easy setting up, especially useful for one-man operation. Then put on the stock, plug in the transformer and off we go.

CHAPTER 7
DIORAMA OR LAYOUT?

The next point to consider is how much space you have got available to use as your proposed layout. That is, of course, if you're going to build a layout. You might have already decided that a small number of near-perfect models of your favourite prototype is as much as time or inclination will allow. Therefore, in order to accommodate these, a small display board is all that will be required. If you then add scenery to this to create a small scene, you have the basis of a diorama.

A diorama will have a number of uses, not just to display your finished masterpieces, but it is also ideal for photographing models. As it is small, it can easily be transported to a preferred location, be it out in the country or in the thick of a mainline station, in order to give you the perfect backdrop. This, when coupled with a good base, will result in a very realistic photograph. If you were then to take the diorama system one stage further, you could end up with a complete layout made up from a series of dioramas. If you do it this way, each diorama can be fairly small, say 4ft × 2ft, completed in a reasonably

short space of time and each one could represent a completely different scene.

Taking this theme further, you could end up with a complete railway system of your own with representative modules of main terminus, docks, country branch, marshalling yard, loco depot etc. This is the thinking behind my current 4mm project 'Bevet' which, so far, has the country branchline, the dock and marshalling yard, with the terminus now under construction. This system could also be applied to a group of individuals standardising on a module size. Positioning of the tracks where they cross the end joints allows each member to build his or her own layout. This system is very popular in America and, at one exhibition I attended in Houston, Texas, over 40 modules had been brought together from all over the state, joined up together, and it all worked.

Turning to smaller projects, two display boards I've recently built are used to display my 'O' gauge modern image models. One is even complete with the overhead catenary suitable for the 25Kv electric locos. I covered a standard 2in × 1in frame

Try this as a taster – a Ratio oil depot in N-gauge built by Alan Maynard.

Part of my original 'Bevet' diorama layout, based on LNWR practice, is the country branch.

with a sheet of Sundeala and laid down a number of lengths of track. I made it so that both will join together, as will subsequent bases. After the track has been ballasted with correct sized gravel and the rail sides painted rusty to resemble the prototype, the remaining exposed areas of board are just simply covered up with scenic material.

If you need to sample railway modelling before you tackle a larger layout project, why not try one of the Ratio plastic building kits? These can be built up and made into a small diorama, and an example is shown on page 45. If you don't want to use a natural background, then a backscene can be added to a board at the back. A number of sources produce backscenes for N, OO/HO and 'O' gauges, or you can be brave and have a go at painting your own.

The second diorama 'Bevinton' is based on a port and Victorian seaside setting.

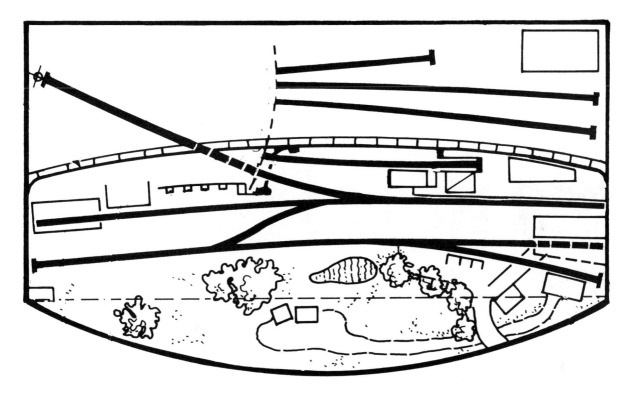

Not all layouts need to be round. This is the simple design for my small diorama layout 'Bevet'. It measures only 4ft × 2ft 6in.

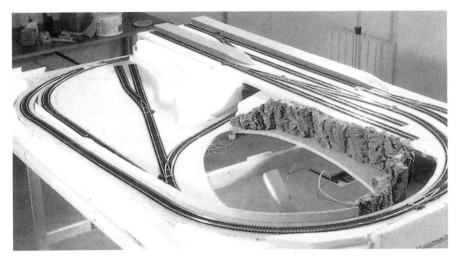

A layout base with the topography added from expanded polystyrene and cork bark. The track is in position as are the top terminus platforms. Make neat cuts on expanded polystyrene with a fine-tooth, saw-edged bread knife (handled with care) or a low-voltage hot wire cutter.

Apply scenic base with neat Polyskim, straight from the pot, available from all DIY and hardware shops. One major drawback with this material is that it is difficult to pre-colour the plaster before use, whereas traditional plaster mixes enable water-colour powders to be added at the initial mixing stage. If the scenery becomes chipped, and no colour has been added, glaring white patches show through the top scenic dressing. Add Peco tunnel mouths at this stage to enable the plaster mix to be faired in around the portals. Splashes can be disguised at a later stage with scenic dressing.

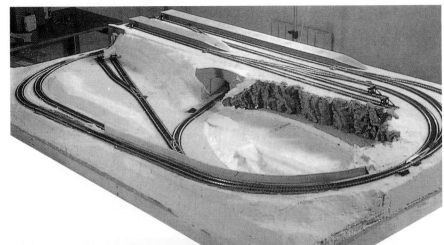

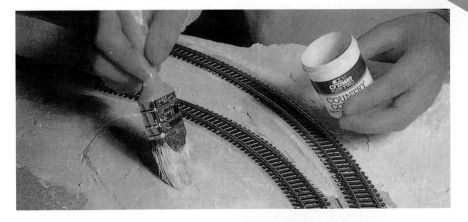

You can now start colouring the landscape. Crown 'Matchpots' are an economic source of emulsion paint and they are available in a variety of shades, but only a few are appropriate to landscape modelling purposes. Emulsion paint is more suitable for polystyrene-based scenic work because oil-based paints will melt any exposed polystyrene areas, or where the plaster is thin and porous.

The two basic shades of paint have been applied over the plaster, and a close examination made to ensure that all areas have been covered and no white patches show through. The rock strata is simply represented by layers of polystyrene which will be dressed with scenic materials at a later stage. The retaining wall in the foreground, on the curve, is made from 3mm ply; this was soaked in warm water to make it supple and follow the track layout.

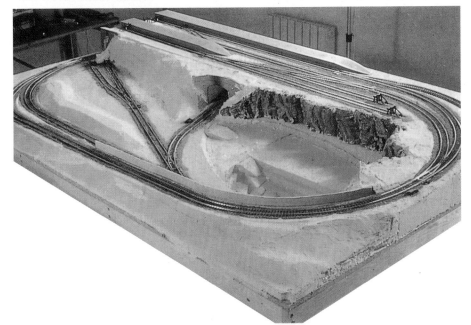

When the paint has dried, coat the whole area to be dressed with scenic materials, covering small areas at a time, with PVA woodworkers' glue diluted in a 50–50 mix with water. In order to make spreading easier, add a few drops of washing-up liquid to the mixture. A glue bottle makes an ideal applicator.

Once the area has been suitably flooded with the adhesive, sprinkle a coarse flock over the whole area; this assists in adhesion when lighter flocks are added later. Apply flock with either a spoon for coarser mixtures or a close mesh tea strainer for finer grades of flock. Disguise cracks in the plaster with scenic dressings as the work progresses. The track is shown ballasted here; this will be shown in greater detail at a later stage in the sequence.

Don't lay too much coarse flock over the adhesive at any one time. Apply the material with a spoon, tapping gently on the side to achieve a uniform covering. Remember, cover only small areas, working a few square inches at a time, so that any glue applied will not have had a chance to dry before the flock is applied. Always take care when using fine particle materials; a mask will prevent accidental inhalation by those who may be working in very confined spaces.

Once the area to be grassed is covered and dry (this can take anything up to 12 hours) the layout should look something like this. You will notice that various shades of green are evident on completion; this effect is entirely acceptable at this stage – it is unnecessary to cover every last square centimetre of painted base. A more realistic effect can be achieved by allowing some of the base colour to show through – it all helps to create the natural look of open countryside.

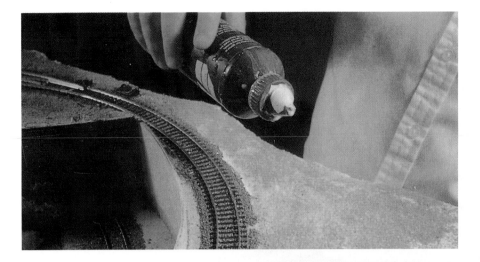

Diluted PVA glue being applied to the coarse flock layer in preparation for finer grades of flock in varying colours which will be added next. Seasonal variations will dictate the choice of flock colour and every season of the year can be represented. Shop around for ready-coloured flocks and what appeals to your taste, because what's available in one shop may not be available in another. All are compatible and can be freely mixed, producing some interesting shades of colour in the miniature landscape.

On this layout, I have used three shades of green. The base green was a fairly bright hue; the two other shades used were a mid and a dark green. The latter shades are of a finer texture, and are shown being loaded into a fine sieve, available from Woolworths as a tea strainer for a few pence.

Blending the colours. The two greens mix automatically as they fall from the sieve, which should be tapped lightly as it is moved across the glued area. If you do not feel happy about mixing both greens haphazardly they can be applied individually, starting with the lighter colour next to the track, working outwards to a darker shade in the field area.

Applying the 'link' colour between ballast and grass. This copies prototype practice, where there is a definite dividing area between the trackbed and the adjoining countryside. Observation of real locations will show area variations of colour and you should always attempt to represent this in miniature. Keep your eyes open when travelling by train or driving in town or countryside; it's surprising how rapidly you will develop an 'eye' for terrain and natural landscape effects, and these will be invaluable as sources of modelling ideas.

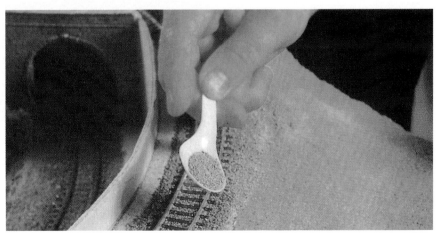

Ballast, dividing 'link' colour and grassed terrain. The 'link' represents the gangers' walkway on a real railway line, and should be a much lighter shade than the ballast found between and to the side of the rails. The ballast receives a large amount of weathering from traffic and this should always be represented in miniature for maximum realism. The retaining wall is ready to be dressed with suitable brick or stone papers . . . or plastic embossed building sheets.

With basic greenery and ballasting complete, it is apparent from the overall view of progress so far, that using such simple techniques rapidly gives an impression of how the model develops from a simple 'train set on the carpet' to a model railway layout on legs, and how easy it can be to achieve this transformation.

There are many 'representations' of trees commercially available. Whether you begin with a simple twisted wire and bristle tree, or go to the other extreme of architectural, hand-built examples, the choice is really only governed by your pocket and, of course, basic requirements. Shopping around you will find suitable types of conifers, etc., such as the ones shown, which are supplied by Orton Models.

Returning to the corner, the outside face of the retaining wall has had several strips of stone wallpaper applied. Moving across the tracks, we can now go on to installing the drystone wall which, with the other wall, forms the boundaries of railway property, as in real life practice.

Using neat PVA woodworkers' glue, straight from the pot, run a good length over the proposed route of the stone wall. Remember, stone walls are not built to negotiate unrealistic gradients, so choose the course the wall will traverse very carefully, and the wall's construction must not look as if it's defying gravity. If in doubt, go and have a look at the real thing!

Using stone walling from Landscape Scenics (which is made from strips of Scotchbrite that have been dipped in glue and sprinkled with granite chippings) results in a very flexible yet realistic model wall. Even though the wall will follow virtually any contour, the rules above still hold good. Follow the run of PVA glue, with the length of wall, and simply press gently into position retaining the wall with household pins until the glue sets. Remove the pins after the glue has dried out completely.

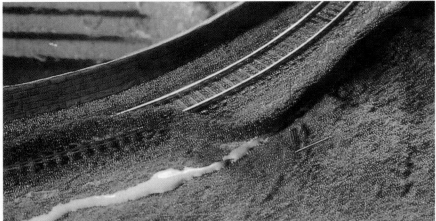

After the addition of trees and walls, the layout takes on another dimension, breaking up the 'flatness' around its centrepoint, and separating the high level terminus site from the lower running circuit. Again, it's a matter of taste as to how many trees are planted, but don't overdo the effect, otherwise the layout could be overcome by aforestation and look completely wrong. Finally, ensure that trees and walls do not foul the running of trains . . . especially if they overhang on the curves.

Using a proprietary brick paper, cover the tunnel retaining walls with one piece and avoid any joins in the brickwork. The effect of retaining walls in a cutting does give a realistic air to the particular piece of countryside in which they are installed. I used Copydex adhesive here because of its curing time; it gives maximum grip, yet ensures plenty of 'slip' to enable the location of brick papers over large areas.

Applying Spraymount adhesive, widely used in photographic and art studios, before the 'highlights' are put on the prepared green base. This particular spray adhesive, although expensive, is very useful to the modeller for work on trees, hedges, ivy etc. It is available from specialist art suppliers and a can goes a long way, if used sparingly.

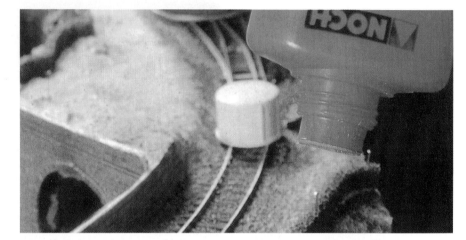

After the Spraymount has been applied, puff on some Noch 'static grass' – short lengths of pre-coloured and dyed nylon fibres available in several different shades, such as medium, light and dark, etc. Using static grass adds height to an otherwise 'flat' terrain.

Above the tunnel mouth, work is in progress on siting undergrowth and bushes. PVA glue, neat and undiluted, is liberally applied to the area to be covered. An attempt should be made, at least at this stage of the proceedings, to cover the required area in one go. Don't worry about excess glue in the wrong places; PVA dries to a clear matt finish and is easily disguised when dried out.

The basis of the undergrowth is rubberised horsehair; this is, as its name suggests, simply animal hair bound loosely in a rubber solution. It is used in the upholstery business, and is available from Scale Link Co., in handy packs for modelling purposes. Cut a piece half the size of the area to be covered; next, gently tease out the hairs to cover the required area, thus giving an airy and open appearance, enabling light to shine through. Too many people make the mistake of depicting such flora as solid lumps and not the 'openwork' structures they are. A small piece of rubberised horsehair goes a long way. Experiment with it before actually committing it to the model.

Liberally spray the positioned rubberised horsehair with Spraymount adhesive ready for the application of Woodland Scenics' foliage. Using this material is similar to working with rubberised horsehair; it consists of minced cellular foam glued to a fibre backing and can be teased out to represent dense or loosely scattered foliage. Again, a little goes a long way, so be sparing in its application.

The Woodland Scenics' foliage in place. Notice how the spacing allows the light to penetrate and show the darker rubberised horsehair beneath. This gives great depth to the foliage and, as a result of two simple steps, produces a realistic hedgerow effect.

After spraying the tunnel portal and edge with Spraymount, darker Woodland Scenics' foliage, again stretched thinly, but this time in strands, is draped on the walls to represent ivy or other creeping vegetation often found on such structures. Just visible in the lower left-hand corner of the picture is the quarry awaiting final touches to complete. This view clearly shows the painted layers of polystrene used in its construction.

Weathering the track. Perhaps the most singularly unrealistic facet found on many model railway layouts is bright, shiny rails! This should really never be seen on a model layout, because it is so easy to rectify. Humbrol make rust colour track paint which is applied with a small brush. Don't worry too much about being 'precise' because rust goes everywhere! Any paint that encroaches onto the top of the rails can be removed with a hard rubber track cleaning eraser.

The control panel consists of an AMR transformer and controller combined. A hand-held unit that can be plugged into the main controller is shown in the middle. This is an optional extra giving dual control, but is not a necessity to the overall operation of the model layout.

The layout in operation, with buildings and accessories in place and trains running.

CHAPTER 8
CONSTRUCTION

While power tools make woodwork a lot easier, ordinary hand tools are equally acceptable. Our basic list of tools is fairly small and I will run through some useful tips when using them. An elaborate workshop isn't necessary – you just need enough room for around 8ft lengths of wood. The tools used include:

Black & Decker Jig Saw
Black & Decker Power Drill
Black & Decker Power Screw Driver
6in set square
12ft steel tape
sharp knife
Evostick wood glue
50 ¾in No 8 screws
100 1½in No 8 screws

Of course there is also the old faithful, the Black & Decker Workmate. To equate power to hand, an ordinary Tenon saw, screwdriver and hand drill will replace the power tools. As to the Workmate, then a small table or even a chair can be utilised, just as long as a G-clamp can be attached

The basic tools required for building the wooden sections of the layout. Power tools certainly make this part of the construction a lot easier.

to hold the work steady. That really is the main advantage of the Workmate – its hold capabilities.

When cutting wood, always mark the line to be cut very clearly with a pencil and

Use a square when marking up the lines. Always cut inside the marked line with the saw.

Pre-drill the holes required in the pieces to be fixed together.

use a square to get the line exact. Also use the square when making joints, as it ensures that the joint is at right angles. If wood is to be interlaced, then once again mark the wood above where it is to be cut very clearly and put a mark on the piece of wood to be discarded. After marking the work, use an off-cut of wood to make the thickness line and measure the half depth to be removed. Cut with the saw inside the lines so that the wood will fit firmly. Clean up any ragged edges with a craft knife. When removing a blind piece, use the knife and score the wood, several light cuts from both sides, and the piece will pop out. Drill the holes to accept the screws in the piece of wood to be attached and start off the screws, then add a slither of wood glue to the other surface. Hold the two pieces together and screw home the screws.

Then slot full length 2in × 1in into the 4in × 1in cross pieces to form a framework.

Check with the square that all is at right angles and, should any adjustments be needed, remove the screws and correct.

It is always best to use both glue and screws in the joints – a good 'belt and braces' job never hurts. We have now finally arrived at the construction stage of the baseboard. I will deal with the standard 2in × 1in framework first, then look at the 4in × 1in version later.

Firstly, construct a frame using three of the 2ft 2 × 1in cross pieces and two of the 8ft 2 × 1in main rails. The cross pieces should fit inside the outer rails, with the overall width the same as the width of the sheet of Sundeala. Do the same with the length, and measure the combined length of two pieces of Sundeala butted up to each other. The front rail should have four half depth cut-outs in it to accept the four extended cross-braces that will support the front curved pieces of the baseboard. Notches in the front rail should face downwards when the frame is assembled. Ensure that the framework fits to the edges of the boards all the way round. Also make sure that the framework is symmetrical, once again using the square for this job. Screw and glue all joints and the Sundeala to the frame.

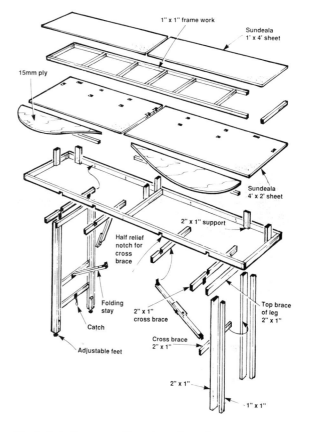

Exploded diagram of baseboard sections.

Lay the trackwork out on top of the baseboard and mark where the trackwork goes.

Check the Measurement!

One very important point when under-taking the woodwork, particularly when measuring and marking a line, is that you should always check the measurement twice, even three times, and then cut only once – it is hard to stick wood back on once it's been cut off. Once the glue in the basic framework and surface has cured (about 30 mins), then add the four longer cross-braces, making sure they fit flush to the board surface. If they don't, then gently trim the notches with a knife so that a good fit results. When you're happy, glue and screw them in place.

We can now take a look at the legs, once again 2in × 1in frame with cross pieces, but this time 1in × 1in lengths have been screwed and glued to the legs. This greatly stiffens the legs, giving more stability. Now for the all-important diagonal folding stays which allow the legs to be folded up or down. Once you have attached the legs, making sure that they will fold one inside the other (see exploded diagram), the stays' measurements can be worked out. When the legs are in the upright position, measure between leg cross-brace and a suitable layout cross-brace, and let's assume that the resulting measurement is 20in. Then fold the leg down to the board and note the relative positions of these cross-braces. If they coincide (lucky), then just halve the stay and add three back flap hinges. If, as is usual, the cross-braces are out, measure this distance. Say it is 4in, then subtract this from the main figure of 20in, result-ing in 16in; this is then halved to give two 8in. Add the 4in to one side, giving two pieces of wood one 12in, the other 8in. Add three back flap hinges and you have a fold-ing stay. Once fitted, fit a smaller piece of wood to the stay secured to one side of the folding stay with screws, and a coach bolt through the other side. This allows the stay to lock-out giving a firm stable base. You now have a free-standing baseboard. Height here is important and I think a baseboard should be at a reasonable view-ing level but this is a choice for the indi-vidual. The front curves are made from 8mm ply, this being a rigid material that won't sag and can be screwed straight onto

A look at the 2in × 1in layout framework showing the supports in position for the upper level.

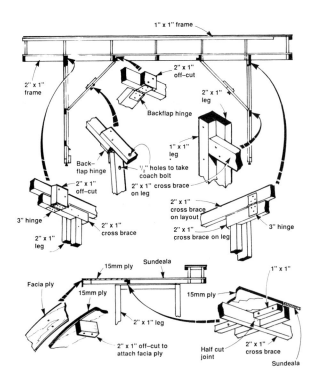

Exploded diagram of various joints used on the baseboard.

Refinements

There are two refinements you might like to add to your layout. The first is a set of adjustable feet. These are made from large 4in bolts with one nut wielded to a large washer while the bolt passes through a door stop held in position by another nut and washer. The second consists of a further cross-brace added to one leg when the legs are in the folded-up position. Line it up with a cross-brace on the main frame and secure it with screws to the leg; then add an eye and catch clip. This will stop the legs dropping down during transit of the baseboard. A carabena clip will secure the catch clip. For a deeper baseboard, use 4in × 1in cross-members with 2in × 1in runners (as opposed to all 2in × 1in construction). This gives a good depth to the layout and allows dual levelling without too much extra work. Following the contours on the model and the areas to be relieved, lowered and channelled, mark out the baseboard accordingly. This is a sheet of 8ft × 4ft chipboard ½in thick.

This skeleton frame is worked out and built up, and it's a fairly simple operation. Notch the cross-members at the corners to take the stretchers and then screw and glue together. When the skeleton frame is complete and has been allowed to dry so it can be easily handled without fear of

the protruding cross-braces. It is shaped to the profile as seen in the photo on the previous page.

We can now look at the upper level which uses a 1in × 1in framework supported on pieces of wood screwed to the main base's cross-braces. These come up through holes cut in the Sundeala surface. The Sundeala surface for this can be cut and screwed on, but not glued as it will have to be removed for the track underneath to be laid. Also note position of the transformer/controller, in our case a twin unit from Tasma. All relevant holes to take the wires for the controllers and point levers are also put in at this point; both through the Sundeala baseboard and the wooden cross-braces on both upper and lower levels. Finally, add small pieces of 2in × 1in wood around the curved edges of the thick plywood at the front; this will have the cosmetic ply secured to them later.

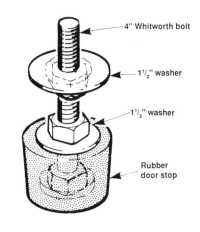

Adjustable foot.

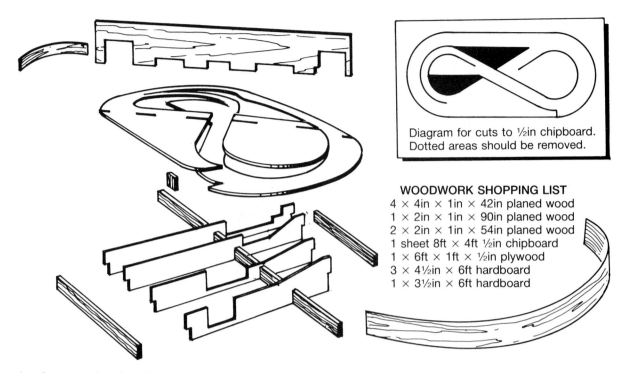

Diagram for cuts to ½in chipboard. Dotted areas should be removed.

WOODWORK SHOPPING LIST
4 × 4in × 1in × 42in planed wood
1 × 2in × 1in × 90in planed wood
2 × 2in × 1in × 54in planed wood
1 sheet 8ft × 4ft ½in chipboard
1 × 6ft × 1ft × ½in plywood
3 × 4½in × 6ft hardboard
1 × 3½in × 6ft hardboard

An alternative baseboard construction uses deeper cross pieces. These can be cut out to allow a sunken track to be used, as opposed to an upper level. By using a single sheet of chipboard the inclines will be more natural.

putting the structure out of square, lay it onto the 8ft × 4ft board. Mark out the board where all the cross-members and joints are located. At this stage, it is a good idea to lay out the trackwork of the board and mark out the principal areas of curvature, intersections, points and sidings. Mark the outsides of the track routes, where the inclines start and finish, where the bridges will go and where the board will be removed and filled out with scenery.

The marked board and skeleton frame are now ready to cut. Here, exercise extreme care – one wrong move and a vital piece could snap off (and it could be painful!). It's only when you look at this operation that you appreciate just how easy and simple a jig saw can make this sort of work. It's a very good investment. Once the framework and baseboard have been profiled, join them together. At this point, you'll find out how accurate your calculations and doodlings have been. The inclines will assume a natural line when

A diagonal backscene will split a layout in half and so can give two different scenes.

Leg units are built to give the layout suitable height and make it free-standing.

fitted to the framework: shallow at the start and finish, fairly steep in the middle. Suitable blocks will be inserted at a later stage to give adequate support. Use screws and glue to fix the board to the frame. Once it is secured, cut and slot the backscene, which is ½in plywood, into the baseboard. Glue and screw and reinforce by ½in quarter round dowelling.

If your layout is going to have a backscene, then first give it a coat of light blue. I used the Crown range of 50p pots, another helpful aid for modellers. The range is extensive and the colours mild and very useful. Once the paint is dry, precisely cut out the backscenes. The cutting out is tedious, but worth it in the end. Now stick the backscenes in place, with the aid of Polycell (wallpaper paste). Leave about an inch clear at the bottom for additional embankments which can be added later.

CHAPTER 9
PERMANENT WAY

Having now achieved a folding platform that should stop your creation from hitting the floor, the trackwork can be laid, centred on the shaped trackbed and located with pins. Here the use of a track pinning tool will greatly speed up the process, and will diminish the disturbance incurred when a hammer and centre punch are used.

On this layout, you can use two ways of ballasting the trackwork. On the running circuits, where there are continuous train movements for prolonged periods, I have used foam underlay. This does cut down the noise. The underlay used is available from Hornby and Peco, although some carving will be required to the Peco point underlays to fit the Hornby points – short underlays for R612 and R613 points and medium underlays for R622 and R623 points. Scale ballasting can also be used and looks very prototypical when added to the trackwork. This does take quite a time to do, but the final effect is worth it.

Carefully spread the ballast (in this case from Woodland Scenics), then, to secure it, use a 50/50 diluted mixture of Evostick PVA wood glue with water. If you add a few drops of washing-up liquid to the mixture, it will remove the surface tension of the water and allow the glue to spread through the ballast easily. When gluing, be careful around the point switch blades, as you don't want any glue in them.

Running Circuit First

Firstly lay down the trackwork according to your plan on the running circuit. Once it's laid out, fit the underlay and pin all the way round. Once this has been achieved, electrify the manual points using R663 Point Remote Control Sets. The electric point motors simply clip to the side of the points and the relevant hole is drilled to take the wires. The upper level board can then be added, and this time screwed and

Using your plan, assemble the track components required for the layout and sort out where they are to go.

Secure the track to the baseboard with pins. A track pinning tool is ideal for this job.

glued into position. Once dry, the track-work can be added. This leaves the link track between the two levels. This will be a mixture of embankment and steel piers, so, to start with, the incline is carefully packed-up using R658 Seven Inclined Piers from Hornby to get a smooth gradual incline. Also used were R659 Three High Level Piers. Embankments will be filled in later.

The only alteration to the rail joints (fishplate) is the reverse loop section indicated on the plan. At the ends of the central section the metal fishplates have to be removed and insulated plastic ones substituted. This will electrically isolate that

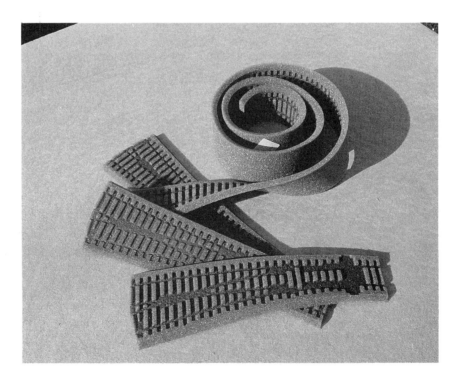

Foam underlay is available from both Hornby and Peco.

Requirements for scale ballasting. PVA wood glue diluted 50/50 with water, a few drops of washing-up liquid, small wide brush, spoon and ballast.

section which will be wired up later. To enhance the track's appearance, paint the sides of the rails and the chairs that hold the rail in place a rust or track colour. This gets rid of that awful bright steel colour.

The choice of venue of the layout will also govern the choice of type of track. I have used Hornby track which has steel rail, as this is more suited to indoor layouts. It would not be too appropriate out in a garage, where it is rather damp and rust could be a problem. For this venue, nickel silver track would be much better suited. This is available from Peco and is a very well-produced product.

Once all the ballasting has been done, both foam and scale, then paint the sides of the rails a rusty colour.

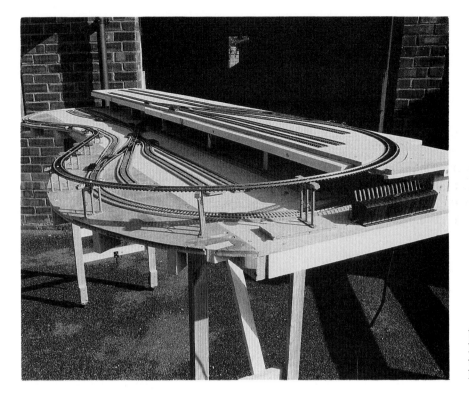

Use a set of Hornby Railways' piers to get the trackwork up to another level smoothly.

CHAPTER 10

WIRING UP

I have deliberately kept the electrics to a minimum, as more and more people I encounter relate their tales of difficult experiences in this area. Having said that, electrics are simple, very flexible, and will enable multi-train movements and, of course, added interest. The terminus, circuit and return loop are all fully isolated from each other by the insertion of Peco insulated fishplates, as shown on the circuit plan below. By using double pole, double throw switches on each circuit, the two controllers can be switched to either of the track sections.

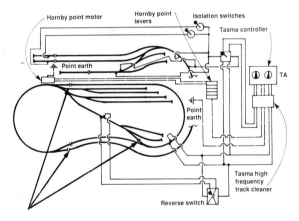

Gaps denote where Peco insulated fishplates should be inserted.

The reverse loop is wired into the base circuit wiring through another DPDT switch, but this time acting as a changeover switch with the following movement taking place. The entrance point is switched and the changeover switch set in the 'down' position and the train enters the centre track and stops at the end. Both enter points are then changed, and also the point for the track up to the incline to the station. The changeover switch is then pushed 'up' and both sections are switched to one controller

which, in turn, is reversed. The train can then move off up to the station. The enter point is then returned to normal, ready for the next train to enter the circuit. Once in the circuit, the two controllers can be returned to separate sections for dual train control.

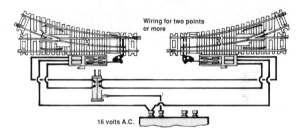

Wiring diagram for Hornby point motors.

Wiring Up Points

Let's now look at the points, with the point motor already in place and the hole already drilled to receive the wires. The point switches (black) are clipped together and are similar to a bank of levers in a signal box. With points nearest to the switches, the wires included in the kit will be long enough to reach to connect both. Simply plug the red and green wires into both the motor and switch.

We can now look at the black lead which is connected to all the point motors. I have run several lengths of self-adhesive copper tape along four of the cross-braces on the main baseboard. The various black wires can then be soldered to them and then a single wire connecting all four can also run to the 16 volt AC supply on the transformer. The other terminal of the 16 volt supply on the transformer connects to the back of the point switches. Test the points for smooth operation and decide on a

The Tasma twin controller is ideal for a basic layout, as it can run two sections simultaneously and also has a separate 16V ancillary supply for accessories.

normal position for the points. If a point direction has to be changed, simply swap over the red and green wires in the point motor.

For those points further away from the levers than the length of the wires provided, you will have to make up new wires. Soldered bullets are available separately from your local model shop, as are the different coloured wires. Try to retain the original colours of green, red and black. Thread the wires through the holes in the cross-braces of the baseboard and cut to length. Strip about ½in off the outer casing, twist the wires and push into the bullet. With a pair of pliers, crimp the ends and then, with a soldering iron, square the bullet with solder.

Two additional electronic boxes can be added to your layout to aid more efficient operation. Firstly, a Tasma twin high frequency track cleaner has been wired into the controller system. This is much easier to wire up than others and it also allows

A spread of points fitted with electric motors, waiting to be wired up ready for operation.

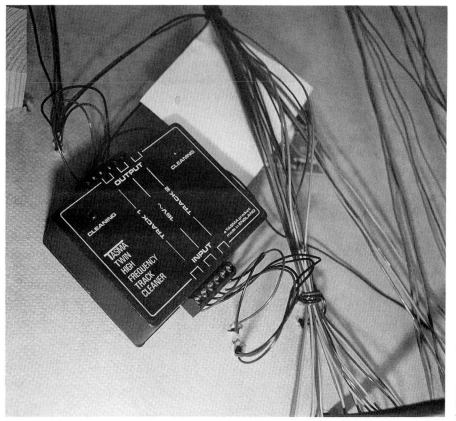

Tasma also offer a Twin High Frequency Track Cleaner, where the wires from the controller are simply connected straight through the unit.

the 16 volt supply that is used to power it to be further used to work the points previously mentioned. Secondly, connected into the point circuit is a capacitor discharge unit. This makes the electric point motors (solenoids) move with more of a thump.

The only other electrical connections to be made are a number of isolating sections on the layout, mainly in the terminus

Wiring has been kept simple. Make the soldered connections to the metal fishplates (rail joiners).

section. These allow the locos that bring the trains in to be isolated and uncoupled from their trains. Another engine can then be coupled to the other end of the train.

The type of switching on the Hornby points allows isolation of a particular road or siding by switching the point to the other road; these are self-isolating points.

CHAPTER 11

ELECTRICS EXPLAINED

Nearly all present-day OO/HO or N-gauge model railways are powered by 12 volt direct current on the 2-rail system, the exception being Marklin HO which uses 14 volt AC and stud contact.

In the 2-rail system, the rails are insulated from each other by the plastic sleeper base. Current flows along one running rail, through the wheels on that side of the locomotive to the motor, and thence back through the wheels on the other side and other running rail. The advantages of this system are realism – in that there are no conductor rails which are not there in the prototype – and the fact that the whole of the locomotive's weight is available for adhesion and contact, no power being wasted in dragging along a contact shoe or skate. This becomes more important as the models get smaller.

Some makers offer the option of overhead current collection on models of electric locos which get their power in this way. However, for the beginner, it is probably best to start with 2-rail anyway; the overhead wiring can be added later and conversion of the wiring is very simple.

Power Supply

The power supply for model railways almost always comes from the mains via a transformer. The use of alternating current mains makes it possible to step the 240 volts of the mains down to a safe 12–18 volts. The AC output of the transformer cannot drive a motor directly (except for the Marklin ones referred to earlier) and so must be turned into direct current or rectified. In addition, control of direction and speed is necessary: these three functions are normally combined in the controller, which is supplied with most boxed train sets.

Permanent-magnet motors are reversed

Always solder wires to the side of the track for the different sections. A small hole drilled at the side of the track allows the wire to be passed through from underneath.

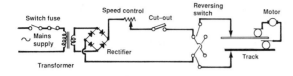

Diagram showing how the mains voltage forming the normal household circuit is reduced to an acceptable level suitable for model railways.

simply by reversing the flow of current; in most controllers, this is done by means of a double-pole two-way switch. The simplest form of speed control is a variable resistance – a length of resistance wire wound on a former with a metal or carbon brush arranged to slide along it – connected in series with the motor; this controls the current through the circuit and so varies the speed of the train.

The components are drawn as symbols which suggest their function rather than what they actually look like (the rectifier, for example, is probably a plastic blob with four wires sticking out, but the symbol shows the individual cells or diodes as little arrowheads suggesting one-way flow). Wires are drawn as plain lines. This is a sort of shorthand used by electricians to make circuits easier to understand, and it's as well to get used to it. Looking at the above diagram, you should be able to see

how the AC mains is stepped down, rectified into DC and fed to the motor via the speed control and reversing switch.

A cut-out is also shown. This is a magnetic or heat–sensitive device designed to break the circuit if the current rises much above that drawn by a normal locomotive, as may happen, for example, if the rails are 'short-circuited' together by derailed rolling stock or a dropped screwdriver. Many controllers include something of the sort.

Points and Sidings

Most layouts include pointwork and sidings, and here we meet the first real problem with the 2-rail system. At the 'frog', or 'crossing', a rail from one side of the track crosses over one from the other side. They must not touch, or there would be a 'short circuit' – the current from the controller would pass straight from one rail to the other and there would be no voltage available for the trains. In most commercial points, this is dealt with by making the crossing of plastic and fitting wire links under the base to feed the current across the gap. A train travelling fairly fast on either track can pick up

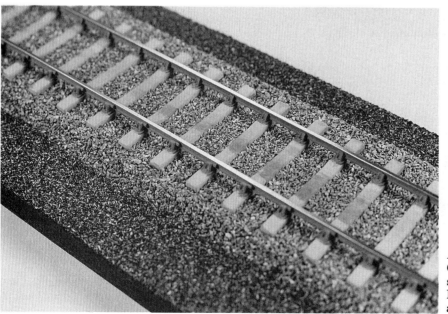

A hand-built track using C&L components for sleepers, chairs and rail. Note the rust finish which adds to the realism.

Basic wiring for a self-isolating point (frog current is switched via the point blades).

current from the wheels on either side of the break, or 'coast' for a short distance if contact should be lost for a moment.

Unfortunately, it isn't that simple. One of the delights of running a model railway is to carry out train movements at 'scale' speeds, making the models move slowly and smoothly to suggest the massive weight of the real thing. At these speeds, however, the model has virtually no coasting ability, and the slightest break in the supply – caused by a spot of dirt or a bit of 'dead' rail – will cause it to stop. In most commercial locos, the wheels are not sprung, and so, however many wheels a loco has, only three are likely to be actually touching the track at any moment. If one of these is on the plastic crossing, the loco will stall.

Several things can be done to overcome this. You can add a flywheel to the motor to enable it to 'coast' farther at low speed, or you can add pick-ups to those wheels of

the loco (especially bogie and pony-truck wheels if it has any) which are not already provided with them. But the easiest move – since it doesn't involve taking locos to pieces – is to use 'live-frog' pointwork.

Live-frog points have the crossing made of metal, but separated from the rest of the rails by insulating gaps. Current reaches the crossing via a switch operated by the lever that sets the points, so that it is connected to the rail of which it forms a part whichever way the points are set. In commercial points, the switching is done by the point blades making contact with the stock rails; a more certain method is to use an electrical switch as a point lever and use it to switch the crossing. The diagram on page 68 shows a way of doing this: the reversing lever is included to make the 'dolly' of the switch point the same way as the turnout setting. Live-frog turnouts are available in both OO/HO and N gauges, though the range is not as extensive as for the dead-frog type.

Point Operation

On a small layout, the points can be set by hand, since they will all be within easy reach for the operator. As the layout gets

Marklin HO track which uses 14 volt AC and stud contact.

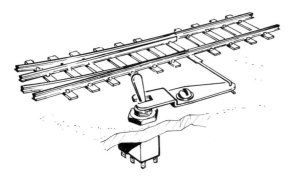

Toggle switch used as a mechanical point lever.

larger – or the amount of delicate scenery such as signals, telegraph poles or overhead wiring, makes it more difficult to reach the track – some sort of remote control becomes necessary.

Point motors usually consist of two electromagnets, between which an iron core slides back and forth. There is usually a locking device – a pin in a lazy-Z slot or an over-centre spring – to prevent the points from being forced over against the setting of the motor. Because the magnets are small, they are not very efficient and require a lot of current to produce enough force to throw the points; if this current continued to flow for more than a second or two, the coils would get very hot and burn out. Thus, point motors are operated by 'passing contact' switches or pairs of push-buttons: the power supply is usually AC taken directly from a 14 volt output on the transformer.

A cheaper substitute for many push-buttons or switches required for a large layout is the 'electric pencil'. A diagram of the layout is painted or taped on a sheet of plywood, hardboard or Formica and, at each turnout, two brass screws are fixed, wires leading from them behind the panel to the point motor. The 'pencil' itself consists of an insulating holder, such as an old ballpoint pen, the refill being replaced by a piece of brass rod or thick wire glued in and provided with a flexible wire to the transformer. Touching the tip of the 'pencil' to the screwheads provides a pulse of current to either side of the point motor, as required. A refinement is a 'holster' in which the pencil can be parked when not in use, to prevent it from making contact with any metal parts which might cause a short circuit.

Wiring Up

So far, we have assumed that the current feed reaches the locomotive only via the rails. This is generally satisfactory in small layouts, where the distance from any

Gaugemaster offer an excellent range of controllers. This one is complete with 16 volt accessory take-off at the back.

point on the track to the feed point is less than 10ft (3m) for OO/HO and 6ft (2m) for N. In larger layouts, however, the resistance of the rails becomes significant, as does the number of fishplate joints if sectional track is used. Some thought should be given to providing additional feeds at intervals, using insulated copper wires of, say, 16/0.2mm or 24/0.2mm gauge, run under the baseboard and connected to the rails by 'droppers' every so often. Ideally, each piece of rail should have its own 'dropper' so that current feed does not rely on the fishplates at all.

A small layout can be built up without soldering, track connections being taken care of by the rail joiners and connection to the rails being via a 'terminal rail' which is usually included in boxed sets. Sooner or later, as the layout grows, soldering will become necessary; there is a limit beyond which fishplates and 'twiddle' joints cannot be relied on. There is nothing to be scared about, for we are dealing with two of the most easily soldered materials, namely copper and nickel silver.

The commonest reason for poor soldered joints is insufficient heat. The iron must be hot enough and have sufficient mass to heat the materials to be joined quickly to the melting point of solder; many small irons designed for miniature electronic wiring do not satisfy this requirement. A 25 watt iron of reputable make, with a small 'chisel' bit, will cover most of the modeller's needs in OO or N-gauge. Put a small blob of 60/40 resin-cored solder on the iron and use it to trap the wire against the foot of the rail, and within a second or two it should be seen to 'flow' onto the nickel silver. Touch the end of the solder wire to the spreading patch of solder, withdraw the iron and hold the wire in place until the solder goes 'misty' – and then for another ten seconds. (The second commonest cause of bad joints is allowing the parts to move before the solder has properly hardened.) The result should be a neat joint, with both rail and wire well 'wetted' with bright solder, but with not too big a blob. Practice on a spare piece of track until you can make this sort of joint every time without overheating the plastic base; it isn't difficult because heat spreads quite slowly through nickel silver.

A similar technique is used for wire-to-wire joints or those between wires and the tags of components such as switches. In the latter case it is usual to twist the wire lightly round the tag to hold it in place

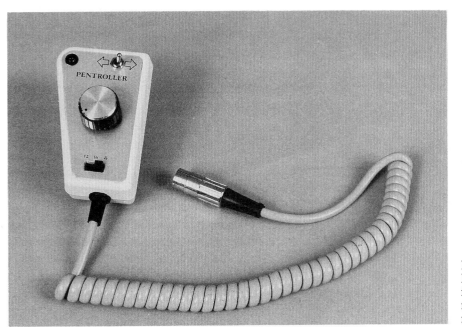

Pentroller by Stewart Hine has been developed for use with iron core motors and Portescap motors alike.

while soldering. Don't twist it too tight —
you may need to take it off again one day!
Feed wires are best brought up through
small holes drilled in the baseboard close
to the rail on the side away from the
normal viewing position, and soldered to
the rail foot. When the track is painted,
such joints are almost invisible.

As the layout grows, the wiring will
become more complex. So that you don't
have to keep this complexity in your head,
start a notebook in which is listed the start
and finish of each wire and its colour. An
orderly approach like this will make it
much easier to repair the system if anything goes wrong.

CHAPTER 12
'DIGITAL' COMPUTER CONTROL

Several years ago, the two major European manufacturers, Fleischmann and Marklin, introduced their respective computer control systems for model railways. Marklin has always been associated with the three rail brush or stud contact. Their railway system is unique to themselves, but the computer control 'Digital' can be applied just as easily to the more popular two rail concept. However, there is no question that Marklin's stud contact system gives better running and reliability overall.

The System

Marklin 'Digital' uses state-of-the-art micro-computer technology. The beauty of the system is that present Marklin layout owners can convert their layouts a circuit or section at a time, by using insulation breaks between the two systems, so they don't have to change the whole lot in one go. However, it is ideally suited to the newcomer who can start straight away with the new 'Digital' HO system.

The locomotive chips or, as Marklin call them, decoders, have eight-function switches, and are easily coded. More importantly, coding can be changed very simply, although the initial fitting of the decodes should be carried out by a recognised Marklin dealer. Even if you have an old Marklin system and want to fit, or are

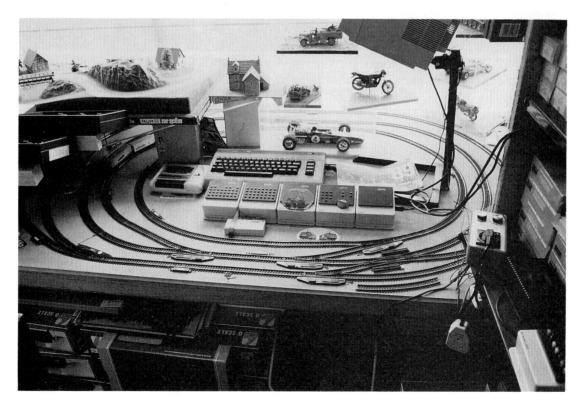

A layout such as this, when fitted with sensors in the track and coupled up to a computer, will run to programmes.

A decoder fitted to a standard Lima diesel locomotive.

thinking about fitting, a decoder-fitted loco, it will still run on a conventional system.

As far as two rail 'Digital' is concerned, the same applies except that the whole layout is converted in one go! However, not necessarily all of the locos, as a loco without a decoder straight out of the box can be run on the system without any conversion. This is done by the same components of control in the system, so that up to 79 locos fitted with decoders and one loco not fitted can be run. A two rail loco fitted with a Marklin chip (6082) can be run on a conventional DC controller ie Gauge-master or H & M etc., so that the owner who has a Marklin 'Digital' two rail system at home can still run his/her decoder-fitted loco on a club layout without damaging the loco/decoder at all. Also, with the two rail decoder fitted, the pre-programmed inertia will still operate on a conventional layout (IEDC).

If more than one (DC two rail) loco is on the digital layout at the same time, then the usual isolating brackets in the rails are used to hold the locos not running, just as in a conventional layout, so it is very simple to convert a standard DC layout to two wire digital operation in small stages.

The main advantage is that, with 'Digital', a non-decoder fitted loco may be run at the same time, on the same track, as a decoder-fitted loco or locos! The transformer unit delivers enough power to handle a large quantity of loco movements and combinations. To get started in 'Digital' HO operation, you will need a Transformer, a Central unit and the Control 80 unit. Plug these into your existing layout and away you go, with or without decoder-fitted locos.

To get a loco into motion, you simply tap in that loco's number and you have control. If you wish to leave that one running at a given speed and move another loco, tap double O and then the next loco's number, and you have control of that one. There is a panic button which will stop everything dead, while you sort out any problem.

One additional function on the Control 80 unit is a green function button which, when pressed, after a loco has been called up, will turn the lights (if fitted to that loco) on or off. Of course, the end which the lights come on is the direction in which the loco will travel – a tremendous help especially with the modern double-ended diesels. Reversing the controller will switch the lights on the other end. Also, locos fitted with the TELEX remote control uncouplers can be activated with this button.

Because the transformer delivers a reasonable amount of power, constant lighting is one of the benefits of this system, and this can be applied to coaches fitted with such units, or trackside lamps can be fed direct from the track. While on the subject of accessories, digital control of switches, signals, uncoupling tracks and any other electro-magnetic accessories can be activated via the track circuitry or by a separate circuit using the Keyboard unit. Each Accessory Decoder can handle up to four switches, ie point motors or signals. It can be installed anywhere on a layout above or below the baseboard. This decoder also has an eight position switch for coding purposes.

Taking this system one stage further, and utilising the foundation heart of the 'Digital' system – the central bus bar system (the multi-pin and socket connections) which connects the various control units and enables communication between them – a device termed 'Interface' has been designed and introduced which will enable a personal computer to be hooked up to the 'Digital' HO system. The possibilities realised by this achievement are almost without limit. With the help of this Interface, a home or personal computer can simulate the currently existing control units (Keyboard, Control 80) as well as any yet to be produced. That is to say, a 'computer freak' can, with the help of the Central Unit, the Interface, and his/her personal computer, control his/her layout as is currently done with conventional transformers and control panels. What is needed for this is an appropriate computer program, which, of course, is available from Frattons (see Appendix A for address), entitled *A User's Guide to the Marklin Digital System* by Dr. Thomas Catherall. This 150-page manual contains an enormous amount of relevant and useful information and costs £15.00 (price current at time of printing).

Route Selection

With route selecting, you can set an entire series of points (for a particular train route, for example) by pressing a single button. This unit is called a 'memory board' or 'routing memory'. With the help

A standard Lima 2-rail loco, in this case a class 33, has had a centre skate added to run on the Marklin studded track.

The British manufacturer, Hornby Railways, introduced a much more basic system, Zero 1, which worked well many years ago. While not manufactured now, it can still be bought second-hand.

of this unit, any conceivable route on a layout with any combination of switches and switch settings in that layout can be programmed to be set with one button. It is possible to program 24 different routes, eight per keyboard, each having 24 switch and/or signal settings, to a maximum of 256, into the memory board. The route selected at any one time will be shown by a Light Emitting Diode [LED] indicator light. Should another route be selected which overlaps the first route at any point, then the original route's LED indicator will blink, thus providing an additional safety factor. When signals or switches are controlled from the memory board, the LED position indicators on their keyboards change automatically, enabling the operator to know at all times the actual status of the switches.

The layout illustrated on page 65 was hooked up to a computer and, with sensors placed at strategic places in the track, a program was set running and the computer literally drove the train through a series of intricate shunting, reversing and circuits, plus, of course, all of the relevant point and signal movements.

No Limitations

This system is so flexible it can be used for every system and scale. Arnold are currently marketing this system for N-gauge. Z-gauge will be covered by Marklin themselves, with LGB as well. It is equally applicable to two rail, as well as three rail/stud contact and, when coupled to a home computer, the system is limitless.

Slow running is very acceptable, and there is currently development work being carried out on Portescap motors. The system is perfect for the layout operator.

CHAPTER 13
SCENICS

Once the trackwork has been laid, wired and found to be working, the next stage is the scenics. This will transform your train set into a model railway, and will create your own piece of history captured in miniature.

The first thing to consider is how you are going to hide the curves at the end of the layout. In order to disguise these, and bring the layout further to life, you should consider working roadways. Faller have just such a system, which needs to be fitted in during the early parts of the initial scenics. Using the roadway as an inspiration for hills, you first have to decide the route the road will take. One single circuit will allow bi-directional working down the

When making the sites for the tunnel mouths, hold a pen against the centre of a coach and mark the baseboard.

main road in the centre of the layout, with single direction working out of the return loop ends.

I decided that it would be nice if the roadway could thread its way around the town outside the station. I also needed the roadway to disappear at the other end so as to make the illusion more believable. When viewed from the front, a large hill rising from the centre towards the right-hand end will hide the roadway, and there is enough room to accommodate a reverse loop.

So, to recap, we have a town scene at one end, using the excellent Hornby Victorian shops and houses, and a large hill at the other end, giving a good view of the terminus on top and the incline and running line below. On the other layout, the country-side is on one side of the backscene and the train terminus is on the other side.

Our first job will be the siting of the tunnel mouths that mark the entry and exit to the scenic breaks, etc. When the track is on the flat, the plastic mouldings can easily be stuck to the base. This will be just below the town, inside the incline and on top above the controls. Where the inclined track enters the hill, an intermediate small base will have to be fixed up, big enough to take the tunnel mouth. The only other entrance is on the reverse curve line and siding, and here a double track tunnel mouth is required. The others mentioned were singles. The small base needed for the inclined track is a piece of ply held up by two off-cuts of 2in × 1in screwed and glued to the baseboard.

Rock Faces

Having now established the limits, take a look at other major scenic features, such

Siting of the tunnel mouths marks the entry and exits of the covered areas.

as rock faces and retaining walls. Rock faces can be easily simulated using cork bark available from the larger florists or garden centres. The ones I have used are, in fact, resin castings that were taken from a rubber mould that I made using a Strand Glass resin casting kit. You can make rock faces that are straight, curved inwards or outwards. This is easily achieved with a rubber mould and allows more flexibility in designing terrain – just support the mould differently when casting. (This is only really necessary if you plan to build a number of layouts.)

The retaining walls are a plastic vacuum forming produced by Langley Miniature Models. Simply trim the wall and lightly tape it in place, then build the remaining terrain around it. The remainder is formed from pieces of polystyrene glued together in layers forming the embankments and hills between the tunnel mouths. I use glue specially designed for use with polystyrene ceiling tiles, available from Texas Homecare stores. I made the base for the town and hill out of shaped Sundeala suitably supported above the lower tracks. The polystyrene is glued to this.

Once the glue has dried (I would suggest a couple of days), then judicious carving of the polystyrene layers can take place. I use

This photograph shows the retaining wall in place along with the tunnel mouth and sub-base above for the next level.

Cut and glue pieces of expanded polystyrene together to form the hills and embankments.

a large carving knife and only take off thin layers at a time; too big a cut and you'll rip the polystyrene. It doesn't have to be a precise finished piece of work, as we will fill in the gaps and cracks with plaster once the

carving is complete. Be careful with the knife, as 'red Martian landscapes' aren't too authentic on British-style layouts (in other words, don't cut yourself – take care with the blade!). Plaster gives a smooth surface to the bulk of the scenery. There should be realistic cracks and crevices for wildlife, such as fox holes or rabbit warrens.

One further area which needs attention is the inclined track connecting the base circuit to the upper level terminus. I initially used the inclined Hornby pieces to give a realistic slope; now a shaped plywood trackbed will need to be marked, cut out and fitted in. Mine was made up of several bits joined together with glue, and a stretcher piece clamped in position until the glue (PVA) is set. Just before gluing in place, shape some polystyrene to fit between the piers then, using polystyrene tile glue and UHU on the piers, stick on the ply base. The track can then be relayed, pinned, ballasted and painted (rust colour on the sides of the rails).

Modelling railways isn't just about trains. It covers the railway environment as well, and that means careful observation of hills, trees, cars, buildings, people, indeed almost everything. After all, the more attention you pay to detail, the more realistic your model railway will become. It's now time to sprinkle a little colour into

Once the glue has dried (allow several days), the hills can be shaped using a carving knife.

Plaster is then used to smooth out the cracks and bumps etc. It also gives a durable shell.

the growing work of art, and here the Crown emulsion paint tester pots are absolutely ideal. Use emulsion which is water-based as it won't attack the polystyrene scenic base. Spirit-based paints will destroy your works of art, not to mention the scenery. Even though the colours are quite weak, they serve the purpose of covering up the great expanses of white. I used a light green for the proposed grass areas, while other areas were painted with a fawn/brown colour.

Paint the Rails

The only other area of paint that requires attention is the rails. As laid, they are a bright steel colour whereas, in prototype practice, rails are rusty. I used Humbrol brick red, liberally painted onto the rail sides using thinners to allow it to spread over the chairs and partially onto the ballast directly underneath. This one operation alone, while tedious, will completely transform the look of the track.

On to the painted landscape. Brush some

The incline is in-filled with pieces of polystyrene with a thin plywood trackbase on top.

Walling and hedges are stuck down onto previously laid lengths of neat PVA glue, and held in position with pins or cocktail sticks until set.

diluted PVA adhesive, that has had several drops of washing-up liquid added to it (this breaks the surface tension and allows the glue to spread quickly), a small area at a time. Then, using a fairly coarse dyed sawdust, sprinkle it over the glued area. Cover the whole of the areas intended to be green with this scatter and allow it to dry thoroughly. The reason for using the coarse scatter is that, under the next layer of flocks to be applied, the base covering will hold a lot more glue as it will be soaked up by the coarse sawdust particles. To achieve an overall grass effect, I mixed three shades of green, then carefully applied it with the aid of a small tea strainer. Don't have one overall green throughout the layout: vary it. Put darker green on steep embankments and lighter greens on the fields. Try starting with the medium green in the centre, the lighter green sprinkled either side, then the final very light green carefully and lightly dusted over the whole lot just to give a highlight effect. With a teaspoon, I applied a link colour, in this case a speckled stone/brown flock, between the greens and along the edge of the ballast.

For steep embankments, tilt the whole of the layout forward or backward so that the area you intend to sprinkle is near horizontal. Rest it on, say, a Black & Decker Workmate, or volunteer a couple of willing helpers to hold the layout while flock is glued and sprinkled on. Do this for the first covering only; subsequent layers should be glued and sprinkled in the normal position, as this will allow realistic layers to build up. Good scenics take time to achieve. It won't happen overnight so be patient, a little at a time.

A further useful item you can add right at the end is some of the Noch electrostatic grass. Using their own puff bottles, the grass (small lengths of coloured nylon) is blown onto a previously glued area – the best glue for this job is photographic Spraymount adhesive. Several small areas will be more effective than large ones.

Rubberised horse hair makes ideal hedgerows. Cut a three-inch strip from the supplied block (Scalelink can supply this item), and tease it out until it's woolly looking. Then, using neat Resin W (white glue wood adhesive), fix to the landscape. Next, liberally coat the bush base and then, using Woodland Scenics' foliage, which again has been stretched out, lightly press these pieces onto the base. Vary the colours slightly and, as a final touch, add a mauve, dark red or even a

A photograph showing a finished country scene. This illustrates the transformation which scenics can make to a basic layout.

pink coloured scatter material in small lumps to represent hedgerow flowers. For ivy around tunnel mouths, use the Spraymount direct onto the brickwork, then apply the teased-out Woodlands Scenics foliage again. Stone walling, available in three-foot lengths, is also applied using neat Resin W and pinned upright until the glue is dry. Scenics is a matter of choice and experimenting. Don't use just one colour, mix several. Be daring and, if you don't like the result, scrap it and try again. You can cover over with different coloured flocks – you just get more depth.

Finally, once all the scenics have been completed, some weathering can be applied to the whole layout, particularly around the track area where dust and spray from the passing trains is deposited on the embankments, trackside buildings, bridges etc. Don't forget the black soot/smoke stains on the centres of the tunnel mouths; once again observe the real thing and then experiment with reproducing it in model form.

CHAPTER 14
TREES

To 'grow' a tree on a model railway layout, the first thing you need is a store of flexible, fine-stranded wire, obtainable from modelling shops or your local electrical contractor.

Having obtained your wire supply, strip it down to bare the wire and you are ready to start. The only tools you need are a Stanley knife, a pair of side cutters or pliers, a pair of scissors for final trimming up and, preferably, a pair of wire strippers. I did without the wire strippers for some time – using pliers and a Stanley knife – but they make life a lot easier and produce less blood-stained trees!

I am not going to specify a wire length for you to start with or how thick a bundle you should gather up – this you must decide by trial and error and by roughly how tall you want your finished specimen to be. However, start fairly modestly, produce a few saplings and gradually build up to medium-sized trees. Leave full-sized oaks and the like until your confidence has built up to a reasonable level. Refer to the photos to see the way in which the wire is teased out and twisted to shape, the most important thing being that, when taking branches off the main trunk (or larger branches), be sure to take the branch through the main bundle of wires so that when the main bundle is twisted further, each offshoot is

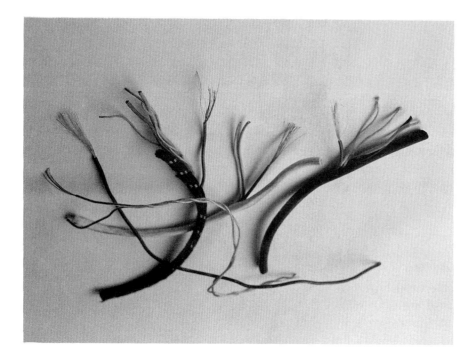

Use any multi-strand flexible wire you can lay your hands on. Examples here include common appliance flex, including some from an iron, and fine-stranded wire used for machine wiring. They must all have technical names, but to the model railway builder they are potential 'wood'.

held firmly as opposed to just falling helplessly away.

If your larger trees are to be removed from the layout, then you need to solder a headless nail or something into the bottom of the trunk, ready to insert into a locating hole in your scenery. I do not bother with this, as I prefer to bed in my trees permanently. I just make the trunks an inch or so longer for the purpose. When you have finished twisting, trim your branch ends to length (where necessary) with the scissors, and plant your masterpiece temporarily into a hole in a piece of expanded polystyrene

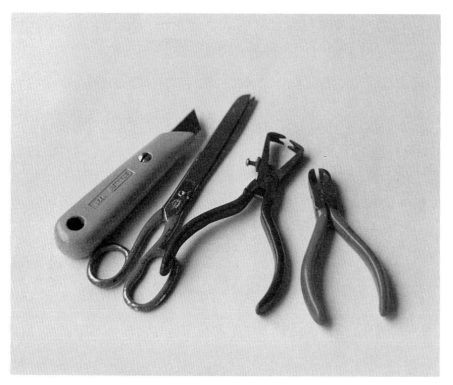

Tools for the job: Stanley knife, scissors, wire strippers and side cutters (pliers are an alternative).

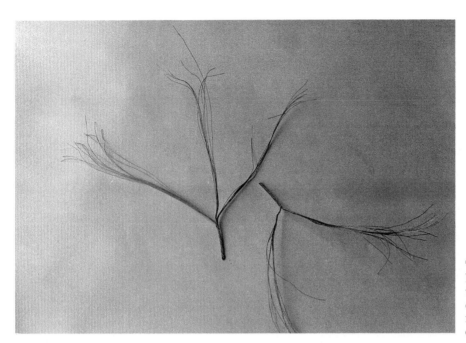

This photograph shows how branches are brought through the main bundle of wire and then twisted further so that the offshoot is held firmly.

where, I can assure you, it will soon be followed by others. Once you have made a start, you will find the habit addictive and you soon run out of space in the expanded polystyrene!

Basic Wire Forms

Having produced your basic wire forms, the next stage is to strengthen and thicken up the trunk and main branches. You can run some solder into them, which helps strengthwise, but this is not essential (especially for a permanent installation) and can be left if the idea is likely to put you off proceeding further. Although you can use a soldering iron for saplings, a gas torch (or similar) is really needed for anything larger.

Thickening up the trunk and branches is now undertaken in the easiest manner that I know. Brush on clay, or wrap with gummed paper if you like (there's nothing

Woodland in the making. A collection of twisted wire forms made during 'tree breaks' at work.

Some examples of twisted
wire ready for covering.

wrong with these methods), but I use a
spray filler from my local car accessory
shop, Spectra high-build Spray Putty
being the particular brand stocked. You
waste some in overspray, but it does not
take many minutes to coat a tree. Should a
fair thickness need to be built up, then it is

best to leave it partly done and put a
second coat on when the first has solidi-
fied. However hard you try, you will get
some unwanted globules on the ends of
branches, but these can be removed when
the filler has dried.

Whatever method you use for this oper-

The spray putty used and
a tree that has just had
the treatment. A further
layer will be added to the
lower part of the trunk
and the wires sorted out a
bit before painting and
application of the foliage.

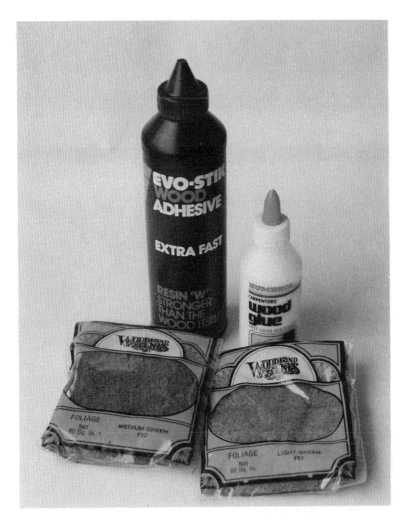

Woodlands Scenics' foliage packs, available from most model shops, and alternative PVA adhesives. The one on the right has a special nozzle for application, but the larger pack on the left can be applied by brush.

ation, the next stage is to paint them. They can be brush or spray painted or, as I usually do, a combination of both. I generally spray (from cans) a primer on any bare wire, followed by an overall colour applicable to the general type of tree I am hoping to create. I then brush paint a bit of variation into the trunk and main branches, making most use of grey and green based colours and keeping clear, for most types of tree, of brown. Preference for type of paint used is largely the whim of the individual, as long as gloss paint is left well alone.

Cleaning pads and loose 'leaves' can be used for foliage, as can commercial products from people like Carrs or C & L Finescale, but I use the Woodlands Scenics foliage matting that is readily available at most model shops. It can work out a bit expen-sive for large trees but it is readily available and easy to use. All you do is tease out the foliage matting, tear off (do not cut, you do not want straight edges) small pieces and glue them to the branches, starting with the bottom branches and working upwards. I dab ordinary PVA woodworking adhesive onto the branches using a small brush, although you can use a modelling-sized container with a special nozzle, but brush application is really the best method. Once the foliage is in place, trim any offending hanging bits or threads with scissors. To vary the foliage a little, spray paint the finished foliage lightly, or spray glue and sprinkle on some loose foliage of a slightly different shade. Your tree is now ready to plant.

Adding the foliage, stage by stage. Start at the lowest level and work up a layer at a time.

Finally trimming off any pieces that look out of place will result in a finished tree.

CHAPTER 15
BUILDINGS

In this chapter, I will discuss station structures, service buildings such as engine sheds and ancillaries, houses and other general detailing equipment.

Once the track has been laid, making sure there is ample clearance for the platforms, then they can be glued in position using neat PVA wood glue. Just run a pencil line along both sides of the platforms, then run the glue down these lines and fit them in place. Secure with several screws through the canopy holes and allow to dry overnight, then the screws can be taken out.

For me, the main feature on this layout is the oval roof. Five units were built up and joined together with plastic weld glue, both along the joining seams and the supports to the platform (it's good glue!). There then remain some unsightly holes in the platform, which should be filled and painted grey after the filler is dry. This imposing structure will become the centre-

piece of the layout, and it will eventually require some careful weathering.

We can now look at the roadways and walling. Faller, the excellent German buildings kit manufacturer, offers an extensive range of embossed pre-coloured sheets. I've chosen the cobbled sheets and the sandstone walling. As they are pre-painted and weathered, you can simply mark them up, cut and stick down using Copydex glue. Firstly, lay out the roadways giving attention to space and accommodating shops and houses that will be built and positioned later on; do not stick them down at this stage. For the tunnel mouth, side walls and other walls around the roadway, the stone walling needs to be marked out carefully, cut, coated in Copydex and applied to the wall. To finish off the walling, there may be a small gap between the top of the walling and the polystyrene scenery that needs filling. I used polystyrene tile glue to fill in this gap.

The platforms are marked on the baseboard, then glued into position, with the unused holes being fitted.

The embossed pre-coloured sheets available from Faller.

Copydex is used to glue the embossed sheets over the guide wires to the baseboard.

Faller Roadway System

We can now install the automatic roadway system also produced by Faller. A very ingenious system, that allows lorries and buses (currently available) to move along a thin steel wire placed in the roadway, it brings a layout to life, as something else is moving other than the trains. Lay down the metal wire using masking tape, then glue down the Faller roadway cards on top, again using Copydex. Take care that, when laying the return loop accommodated in the hill, there is enough clearance around the track and that the circle is not too sharp or the vehicles won't be able to negotiate it. Returning now to the town area, lay the wire in the previously marked sheets, making sure you allow for vehicles to slew out round sharp corners. Check that the vehicles move around the circuit properly, then glue down the roadways. While this system can be expensive, it is worth getting and laying the wires early in the construction under the roadway rather than ripping up all your hard work later.

Part of the roadway sticks out over the centre tunnel mouth, so some sort of beam is needed to represent a support. I used two

Retaining wall, again
from card, is fixed to the
polystyrene with Copydex
and any gaps filled.

lengths of Peco N-gauge station edging upside down, glued together then glued onto the edge of the Sundeala sub-base. The retaining wall should also be spray-painted. This can be simply done using a piece of card cut to shape as a mask, then a small dark grey minispray aerosol can be used to spray paint it. Be careful of overspray.

The houses and shops used for the town are available from Hornby. They are injection-moulded kits which make up into

Hornby Railways
building kits were used
for these 'semis'.

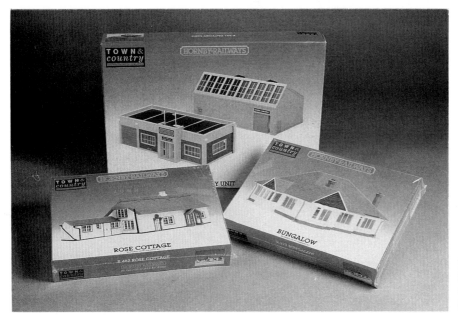

The range of Hornby kits is extensive. Shown here are factory units, cottage and bungalow.

good representations of Victorian buildings, and they are well detailed. Simple conversions can be carried out to give varied formations. The final painting, given care and patience, will result in very attractive models. They are complete with gutters, doors, curtains, front walling and basic interior walls and stairs. Other details can now be added to the layout, including telegraph poles, lineside huts,

From my layout, a scratchbuilt station building with individual roof tiles, platform slabs and brickwork. The effect is convincing but it is also time-consuming.

EFE cars are excellent value as well as faithful replicas of the real thing.

and even a TPO set (travelling post office). As I said earlier, it's the details that make for realism.

The main wall around the perimeter of the upper level mainline station is made from a Wills retaining wall kit. Cut two strips of walling from each of the walling sheets about 32mm deep in 4mm scale, or 8ft high in real life. Glue the two pieces together, add the buttress pieces either side at one end only, then the top stones along the length and the cap on top of the buttress. Glue the sections in place together using polystyrene glue and to the baseboard with UHU. Later, it should be painted and again lightly weathered. While on the subject of finishing off, I always like to finish the edge off around the front and sides of the layout with thin plywood shaped to the contours of the baseboard. Nice flowing lines at the front make a model railway set-up more attractive to the eye.

Langley Miniature Models' generator lorry forms part of their Fairground scene.

Even though we've put a moving roadway on the layout, you will still have room to place parked cars, lorries and buses etc. The best range for the OO modeller is manufactured by EFE. These diecast vehicles are superbly detailed and very accurate. If you want to be clever, you

The range of EFE lorries is very extensive; here are just two examples.

These EFE lorries have had alternative cabs fitted.

While the continental models are made to the smaller HO scale, they are suitable for the back of layouts – a bit of perspective modelling.

Corgi and Dinky sometimes produce vehicles to a usable scale. This one is for 'O' gauge.

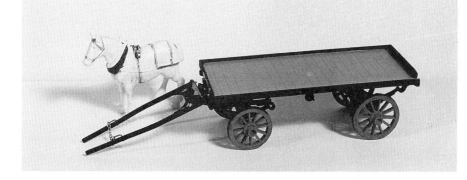

The traditional horse and cart will be more at home on earlier period layouts. This Slaters' kit is for 'O' gauge.

route the wires for the Faller 'car system' round, say, a bus that has pulled into a bus stop or a car that may have broken down or a delivery lorry: the possibilities are endless. To complement this range, Langley Miniature Models offer some cast white metal kits. They even supply alternative cabs to suit the EFE lorries.

A scene from one of my LNWR layouts shows how a small area can include a high degree of detail.

Johnson Great North of Scotland No.92 The Great North of Scotland Railway placed an order with the private locomotive builder Neilson of Glasgow in 1893 to build nine of these small tank engines for use on their suburban services out of Aberdeen. The engine illustrated is a 7mm to 1 foot, fine-scale electric model, constructed throughout in nickel silver, and was hand-made to special order, with only the Swiss electric motor being bought in. The original Neilson Works drawings were used as the basis for producing an accurate model.

GWR 5567 The Great Western Railway built 175 of these little tank engines for branch line service from 1906 onwards. In use on light passenger and freight trains, they could be found throughout the system until their duties were taken over by diesel traction. Today, these popular machines can be seen at many railway preservation centres, from the Midlands down to South Devon, still earning their keep as working engines. The engine illustrated is a 7mm to 1 foot fine-scale electric model, hand-made by Vic Green.

Stanier 8F 8097 The London Midland and Scottish Railway's premier heavy freight locomotive was the class 8F 2–8–0 built under the direction of Sir William Stanier. This engine was a direct descendant of the Great Western Railway's goods locomotive of the same wheel arrangement. While capable of hauling heavy mineral traffic, the engine was also suitable for fast freight trains. Even the occasional passenger train would be seen with an 8F at the front.

During the Second World War the design was selected for use by the War Department and, in addition to those built by the LMS, a large number were built by private locomotive builders. In Army use they saw service in the Middle East. The design was also taken up by the wartime Railway Executive and built in the workshops of the railway companies as a standard freight engine for use in this country. In all 852 engines were built.

The engine illustrated is a 7mm to 1 foot fine-scale electric model hand-made for Gauge 'O' by Vic Green to the order of Kiril Grey of Shrewsbury.

Above: **Stanier rebuilt Scot 6115** In 1927 the London Midland and Scottish Railway was in urgent need of a powerful express passenger engine for working its prestige Anglo-Scottish services. Fifty engines were ordered from the North British Locomotive Company of Glasgow, and in 1930 a further twenty were built by the LMS themselves at Derby.

These engines with 3-cylinders, 6'9" wheels and a parallel boiler became members of the Royal Scot class after the first engine. In 1933 a Royal Scot was sent to Chicago to take part in an extensive tour of North America before returning to this country to take up the duties for which it had been designed. By 1942 the engines were in need of attention due to their very heavy usage and the Chief Mechanical Engineer of the LMS, Sir William Stanier, decided that they should be rebuilt with taper boilers, new cylinders and larger tenders.

6115 *Scots Guardsman* was the only rebuilt engine to be fitted with smoke deflectors by the LMS and it was not until the engines were under British Railways ownership that the remainder of the class were fitted.

The engine illustrated is a 7mm to 1 foot fine-scale electric model hand-made by Vic Green to the order of RJH Model Railways Limited of Poole for use on the very fine model railway of the late Colonel Ronnie Hoare. The fully detailed model *Scots Guardsman* was painted in 1946 livery by Alan Brackenborough. The real *Scots Guardsman* together with *Royal Scot* are both preserved.

Right: **Merchant Navy Class Clan Line 35028** When Oliver Bulleid was appointed to the post of Chief Mechanical Engineer to the Southern Railway, his first new design was for a three-cyclinder Pacific for heavy passenger duties. The 30 air-smooth original engines were built over the period 1941 to 1949 in the Company's own workshops at Eastleigh. Seven years after the last engine was built, the first rebuild of the class entered British Railways service and within three years all of the class had been converted to the form pictured here.

The engine illustrated is a then-unpainted model of one of several engines of this class – *Clan Line* – which have been preserved, and is owned and operated on rail tours on the BR main line by the Merchant Navy Preservation Society. The model was hand-made in 7mm to 1 foot scale by Vic Green.

Further working preserved engines of the class can be seen at other preservation centres in this country, and a sectioned-restored *Ellerman Lines* can be examined at the National Railway Museum, York.

Above: **Stanier Jubilee 5690** The Jubilee locomotive class was Sir William Stanier's first 4–6–0 express passenger engine built for use on the London Midland and Scottish Railway from 1934. Totalling 191 machines, fitted with 3-cylinders and 6'9″ driving wheels, they were to be found throughout the LMS from Bristol to Glasgow, Liverpool to Leeds and south to London.

The engine illustrated is a 7mm to 1 foot, fine-scale electric model. Constructed throughout in nickel silver, with every part hand-crafted from the original builder's drawings, and painted by Alan Brackenborough, the model represents *Leander* as it was in the late 1930s.

Right: **Stanier Class 5 44874** When in 1932 Sir William Stanier took over the post of Chief Mechanical Engineer of the London Midland and Scottish Railway there was a pressing need for a mixed traffic engine, a type capable of working fast freight or express passenger trains throughout the system with equal efficiency. Stanier had been Principal Assistant to the CME at Swindon on the GWR, and it was natural that he would loosely base his own engine on that of Swindon's Hall class which fulfilled a similar function. A total of 842 engines of this type were built.

The engine illustrated is a 7mm to 1 foot, fine-scale electric model, hand-made for Gauge 'O' by Vic Green. Constructed from nickel silver throughout, with all patterns and castings made by the builder, the model was painted in British Railways livery by Alan Brackenborough.

Right: The current West Coast Main Line traffic is hauled by 25Kv electric locos that draw their power from the overhead catenary system. This is efficient, cost effective and clean. This was the form of power that BR were aiming for when they decided to finish steam on British Railways. Pictured here are my models of three classes which span the electric era. Left is the current, state-of-the-art class 90; centre is the oldest member, the class 85, now down-graded to secondary duties, such as stock movements; and, finally, the class 86 which along with the class 87 have been the main stay of electric motive power.

Left: The second electric loco I ever built was 86 401 *Northampton Town* in the very striking Network SouthEast livery. As a spraying and masking exercise it really was a challenge, and involved six reverse masking stages. That's when the colour is sprayed on first, then masked out; the next applied, then masked out; and so on. Once again, extreme care has to be taken, as all the lines must be absolutely straight and equidistant or they stand out! As these models represent the full size, I weather them realistically using both paints and weathering powders.

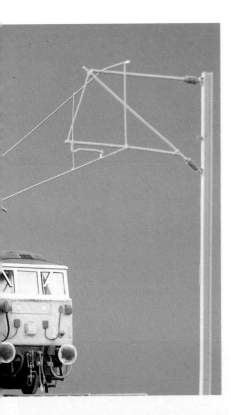

Above: A class 90 in profile shows the smooth lines of the latest design. The loco, built by me to 7mm standard, is in the triple grey Railfreight livery showing sub-sector designation of RFD or better known as 'double diamond' by the drivers. Note the radio aerials just behind the cab roof. All these models are built using RJH kits.

Far left and left: The most recent model I've built has been of a class 59 diesel in the latest private owner livery of ARC.

These locos, built by General Motors of USA, were bought by two private aggregate companies in this country who have heavy trains on BR. Although privately owned, they are driven by BR drivers. These very striking locos are very powerful both in character and reality, and both versions are available in kit form from RJH Model Railways in 7mm scale.

British Rail Civils have recently gone through a number of livery changes culminating in this one, called 'Dutch' livery. The striking broad yellow band down the side makes this stock really stand out, particularly when seen in a block train of vehicles. The loco is a class 47 diesel that is dedicated to Civils or, as it is better known, 'permanent way'. A lot of the loco depots have their own motif which is displayed as a cast plate on the cab side. The springing cat seen here is for the Crewe MPD. Also featured here are two pieces of rolling stock used by the Permanent Way gang.

The hopper-like vehicle is called a 'Sealion' and internally has two compartments which have three operating doors underneath. They carry ballast for the track which can be dropped either side or in the centre as required. The other vehicle is a 'Shark' brake van, fitted with full width ploughs, that can be lowered down close to the track and spread the ballast that has been dropped by the 'Sealion' wagons. All three models are from RJH Model Railway kits, built by myself for British Rail.

Two views taken from my original 4mm scale LNWR layout 'Bevleys'. Over the years, this has been awarded eight trophies for achievements in stock, scenics and trackwork at some of the top model railway exhibitions. Built to P4 standards (more exact scale than OO/HO) it is a freelance location based on LNWR practice at the turn of the century

Top, a K's Milestone 'Lady of the Lake' kit has been motorised giving a very attractive, elegant looking loco. The key word to my modelling is detail.

Right, a Jidenco 'Coal tank' runs into the final extension with a rake of vans both four and six wheel. I built the trackwork with plywood sleepers, with copper rivets punched through and the rail soldered to it; then I glued white metal castings either side of each rail to represent the chairs that hold the rail. The gnome on the signal is a built-in 'gremlin' and has become my trademark.

One of the layouts whose construction details are given in this book. Based on ready-to-run stock and components, it shows how the addition of scenery can transform an OO/HO train set into a model railway. The central backscene running diagonally across the layout divides it into two, giving completely separate scenes.

A scene from Roger Nicols' N-gauge continental layout 'St Niklon' shows just how much realism can be captured even in the smaller scale. Most of the fittings, accessories and stock are readily available, and the effect is very convincing when flared into the scenery along with a good helping of trees.

Up to 'O' gauge scale, and this view shows part of a layout which is some 30 feet long. Here the scenics are on a massive scale and they blend into the backscene superbly. This layout is currently on display at Slater's, Matlock Bath, and is well worth a visit. It depicts the Midland mainline in its heyday in the early years of the twentieth century. This is 'Millers Dale', the large interchange station on the Peak Forest Line.

CHAPTER 16
HINTS AND TIPS

In order to run a successful model railway, some basic areas need attention now and again. Like any large machine, a good oiling now and then keeps it moving. Cleanliness is the key word to the successful *running* of a model railway. I emphasise 'running', as it is very easy to obtain a large static layout and is so hard to maintain an even, smallish fully-working layout. Both track and locos should be cleaned regularly.

After solder, and in particular flux, has come into contact with the track, ie the soldered electrical connections, always make sure that there are no soldered areas on the rail. If there are, file them down, but be careful not to damage the rail surface, otherwise rusting/corrosion may set in at a later date. Clean thoroughly the track with a suitable abrasive rubber, such as those from Fleischmann or Peco. Where glue from the scenic application may have set on the rail surface, the rubber will show it up. Those areas should be chipped off and then cleaned with the rubber. Subsequent cleaning can be undertaken using

meths which if used regularly will eliminate excessive use of the abrasive track cleaner. Meths can be applied with a rag, preferably fluff free, or a track cleaning car or loco.

Loco wheels should also be cleaned at regular intervals, scraping off any stubborn muck with a small screwdriver, then use a glass fibre pen (also used in cleaning electrical circuit boards). Stock should only need occasional cleaning. Application of oil to loco axles, motors, gears etc. should be very sparing. Don't allow any moving parts to go dry, so keep them lightly oiled. Also remove any fluff or dirt that may have accumulated around the moving parts, such as axles, wheels etc.

I have already mentioned soldering electrical joints. This subject holds many fears for a lot of modellers. There are basically two different temperatures of soldering applied to different materials. These are the normal 4-core soldering and then the more specialised, but very relevant to model railways later on, white metal soldering. Both require the same basic technique.

Keeping the track clean is the single most important job – a good track rubber is an essential.

When using two-part epoxy resin mix up a small quantity on a spare piece of card and then apply small amounts with a probe.

The correct soldering iron is crucial for the right job. I would recommend an Onyx iron for 4-core soldering; both the 45 watt and 60 watt in their range are ideal. I work on the basis of getting heat into the job, allowing the solder to flow, and getting the iron out.

Cleanliness is the key word in soldering, and a good flux is equally important. Both items being soldered together must be clean. Flux them both liberally, then bring the soldering iron loaded with solder to the joint; the solder will easily flow after which quickly remove the iron. The joint is almost instant; in the same way, the items can be separated by first fluxing and then re-introducing the soldering iron. When dealing with white metal, a special low temperature controlled iron is required. The one I would thoroughly recommend from personal use is available from Litesold.

Gluing

While on the subject of fixing things together, we must take a look at gluing. There is a vast array of glues on the market to do any amount of jobs. All I can do is to list the ones I use and the applications I use them for. The most universal is UHU, a multi-use glue for many applications. Be careful when applying it, as it is

stringy, so, when applying, make sure the stringing doesn't go everywhere. On the layout, I used it to stick the tunnel mouths to the board, and plastic walls to the base, indeed any time that two unlike materials need to be joined. It is ideal for metal, wood, glass etc. For joining like materials, I use Evostick PVA woodglue for wood, Copydex for gluing cardboard to several different materials such as wood, and even polystyrene tiles. Polystyrene tiles are glued together with polystyrene tile glue available from Texas Homecare. And then there is superglue. There are now so many various types and makes on the market to do every conceivable job, that it is difficult to know which is the best, let alone afford the expense to try them all. Superglue will shatter if the items joined together are dropped. The one I use, again only a personal preference, is by Loctite. It also comes in a single drop dispenser tube, which means it lasts longer before it clogs up.

When using any glues where only a small amount is required on a joint, squeeze out or mix up a small sample on a scrap piece of card or wood and then, using a cocktail stick, apply sparingly a small amount of glue to the required joint. Whether you are gluing or soldering, hold-

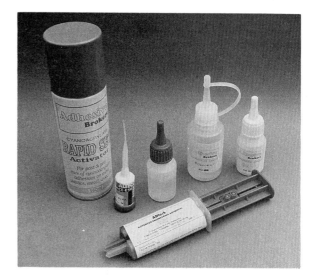

Superglues come in various types and quantities, this set includes thin superglue for adding fine detail, two-part epoxy resin for metal kits, thick superglue for fillets and rapid set for quick setting.

ing the items to be joined together is another key factor to a successful strong joint. For example, when gluing two pieces of wood together, once the glue has been applied and the pieces of wood joined, place a suitable clamp around it and within minutes the joint will be strong, although it is best to leave it overnight, or better still 24 hours, to harden off. Apart from the superglues where the joint is almost instant, most glues take a time to cure, preferably 24 hours. There are many clamps available to do most jobs, and then there are some you will have to adapt yourself to do awkward jobs.

When undertaking modelling, you don't have to own a complete workshop – a range of simple tools is all that is needed to make a start. I mentioned at the beginning of the book the basic tools required for woodwork. For modelling, the list is also fairly small, although my range of tools has grown over the years as I've acquired more sophisticated tools to help do the simple jobs better and more accurately. Such things as a lathe and milling machine weren't essential in the beginning, but they have now become to me another right arm. A firm base to work on is always preferable. I have a piece of plate glass on top of a suitable desk. Choose a comfortable working height and, most important, a comfortable chair. Next is a cutting mat, which allows the knife to cut through the

The Buffalo drill from the Minicraft Black & Decker range is a very useful aid. A separate transformer is required.

material you're cutting and into the mat, but won't blunt the blade so easily as if you were directly cutting onto a hard surface. The knife I use is one by Edding and has blades that can be snapped off – five new edges per refill – a lot easier than unscrewing the handle and fitting a new blade when you're right in the middle of a cut.

Straight Edge Cutting

When cutting, a straight edge is important so a good metal ruler is ideal. Six inches long is adequate, 12 inches ideal. Also most definitely required is a 4-inch engineer's square. In this hobby, anything not square stands out like a sore thumb so get it right from the start – nice and square. A decent HB pencil and a metal scriber are required along with a couple of Swiss files (here I use a rat's tail and a fine triangular), several different paint brushes, tweezers, a fibre glass pen with refills and finally an electric drill with accessories. It is this last item that has the most uses when used with a range of various attachments. Black & Decker market the Minicraft range of tools ideally suited to the modeller. A hand-held Buffalo electric drill with a variable speed transformer is a lifetime's investment. Useful attachments that I would recommend are a circular saw, graphite disc and diamond impregnated

Basic tools needed for a simple kitchen workbench. Cutting mat, knife, files, fibre pen, tweezers, steel rule, scriber, hand drill and superglue.

rubber wheel, all on their own arbours, plus a number of routers and a good set of numbered drills.

The three main attachments mentioned as ideal are as follows: the circular saw will cut plastics, wood, etc; the graphite disc will cut through any metal section particularly rail, ideal for isolation gaps; rubber wheel is excellent for rewiring solder from brass and routers to machine away plastic, white metal etc. As you can see, they are very useful and important additions to the modelling workshop. You should also keep several types of glue, say UHU, superglue and two-part epoxy.

When drilling a hole, start with a small drill first as a pilot, then step up in drill size to the actual size for the hole you require. Don't make a drill chatter or do too much work – you'll shorten its life by blunting it.

When cutting, draw the knife across the line lightly first, holding it close against your metal edge, then increase the pressure slowly on each successive pass, until a complete cut is arrived at. When gluing, do it sparingly; build up in small amounts, rather than a sudden rush from the tube (when you press too hard) that runs everywhere and ruins the job. Keep your working surface clean. Give yourself room with the various parts laid out in sequences of construction.

Finally, take care of your tools and they'll last. Before filing, run the serrations through talcum powder to stop metal clogging the cutting surface, and make up a useful stand for the flux bottle and drill bits. Keep the soldering iron tips clean by wiping muck off of them with a rag and then re-tin it each time. As this is done when the iron's on, *be careful*.

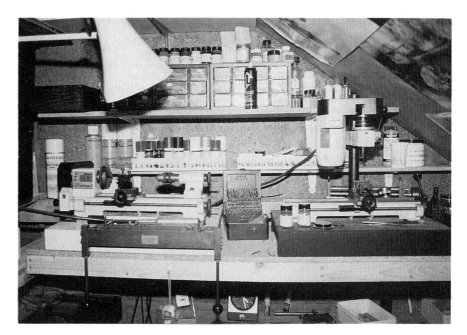

A workshop such as this isn't required from the outset, but it does make life easier later on.

CHAPTER 17
TOOLS

To expand on the previous chapter, before even contemplating any sort of conversion or kit building, you must first equip yourself with a selection of hand tools. These needn't be expensive, although you do get what you pay for. So, if you buy wisely from the start, the tools will still be there after a long period of time, and you'll find the more you use them the handier and more adaptable you'll become with them; after all, practice does make perfect.

Craft Knife

There are numerous variations of this tool. It is by far the single most important tool, coupled with a steel ruler. Illustrated on pages 102–104 are a number of variations stocked in high street model shops in most local towns. The type, style and shape are entirely up to the individual, and it is best to visit a shop and try out several to find one that suits.

Bear in mind when choosing that the blade will wear out and replacements will obviously be needed. Also check on the ranges of different types of blades, as a selection of shapes will be useful for different styles of cuts. I use a heavy Stanley knife for cutting thick materials, while a Swann Morton scalpel is better suited to etched brass fret tags and cutting lighter materials.

Cutting Surface

While this isn't a necessity at this stage, once you've bought one it's there almost for life. I am referring to a cutting mat. Proops Brothers market an Edding CM30 cutting mat which not only prolongs the life of the blade but also allows a stable cutting surface, and it can be used to cut materials square as it incorporates a 5mm grid.

Finally, Woolworths do a superb range of plastic drawer assemblies that are

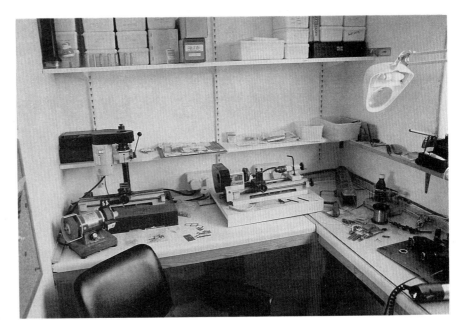

The layout of a good workshop is important. Space is always at a premium so use it wisely.

4in. engineer's square, 6in. steel ruler and scriber.

ideally suited to the modellers' little pieces and the cost here is very acceptable. A point worth mentioning is the subject of stock boxes and here again Woolworths sell a nice piece most suitable for this job – metal toolboxes. Either single tray or multiple-tray types are available and the cost again is reasonable. Not only are they just about the right size for trains (here I'm talking about OO/HO models), they are also extremely strong.

Straight Cutting Edge

Colloquially known as a 'ruler', these are again available in a variety of shapes, sizes and, of course, materials. Here again, the various types have their uses. The most commonly used is probably the engineer's steel six-inch ruler which is calibrated in both inches and mm/cms. These are also available in 12 and 18-inch versions, possibly a little big for our type of work. Plastic rulers are ideal when using a bow pen to line out a loco, or if a source of reference is needed when drawing straight lines, while wooden rulers are quite definitely a major requirement when building soldered track – the plastic ones tend to melt!

For cleaning up metal after soldering, these fibre pens and stick are excellent.

Files

A pack of six Swiss files will give you the various shapes and sizes needed to move a

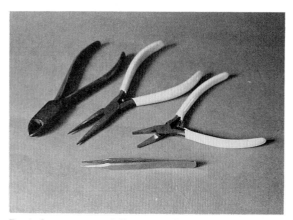

Basic long nose and flat nose pliers, tweezers and cutters.

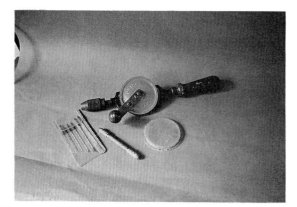

Holes are made with drills. Reamers are invaluable to enlarge small holes.

lot of metal quickly, while the smaller files clean up and finish off the job.

Tweezers

A small pair of steel tweezers is essential. Several types are available – some are of the self-grip type, others require finger pressure to hold the object. These are ideal instruments to be used when locating small fittings and holding small components when soldering.

Clamps of any size and shape are helpful during construction.

Pliers

There are probably more versions of this piece of equipment than any other item, except files. The main type that I use extensively is a pair of small nose pliers, a 'meatier' pair of the same sort and a pair of side cutters. But the range is such you could have one pair for each day of the week. A selection is shown and these are available from Proops Brothers.

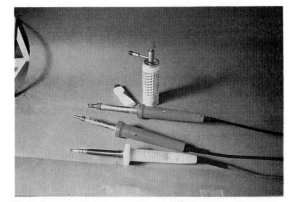

Heat is supplied by various soldering irons, with different heat ranges. The mini blow lamp is used on thicker metal.

Screwdrivers

Here again a selection is useful, and the range is there to choose from. Basically, a flat-ended small and medium and a small crosshead will suffice.

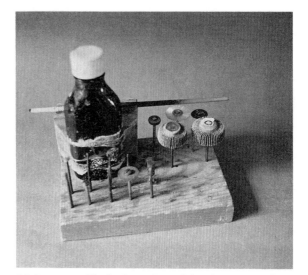

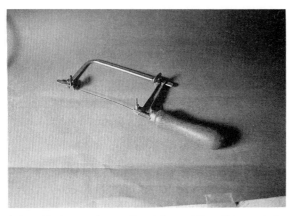

A jeweller's saw is excellent for cutting thin metal.

Make yourself a little toolstand for the various bits for a small electric drill. The bottle contains flux for soldering.

Scissors

A small pair of sharp scissors is ideal for cutting out etched brass frets. Again, from personal choice I use the pair included on the Swiss army knife, although small nail scissors will do just as well.

Drills and Drill Bits

A small hand drill with suitable drill bits can be an expensive investment; a set of numbered drills is also costly. The drills involved range from No. 1 to No. 60 and then, as another set, No. 61 to No. 80, the latter being very useful to modellers. To accommodate these smaller drills a pin chuck is required, which can come complete with several different sized collets; types vary according to manufacturer.

Micrometer and Drill Size Card

While these are not essential, they really do make life much more easier. Using the micrometer to measure the wire or item for which the hole is required, loop up the diameter measurement on the dial and read off the correct drill size. These items are available from the more specialised tool shops.

A small riveting tool gives consistency.

Jeweller's Saw

In order to cut metals, plastics and even white metal castings, this saw is ideal, providing a good range of blades is also purchased. For example, soft white metal would need a coarse blade that won't get clogged too easily. Whereas, for brass, a finer-toothed blade is required. Again, this is available from the more specialised tool shop.

Vice

In order to carry out all the filing, cutting and mutilating, a good base is required to work on. Various vices differing in shape and size are available. One with multi-angle movement is more suited to the modeller. In a similar vein is the special V cutting plate, which is something to be acquired at a later date.

Calipers

While I would put these in the 'not essential' section, when serious modelling takes a grip, they will become necessary.

Set Square

In the same category as the above is a small four-inch engineer's set square – invaluable.

G-Clamps

Again available in various sizes, are certainly very useful, the smaller two to three-inch ones are ideal.

So to summarise the essential requirements, we have:

Knife – ruler – set square
Swiss files – rasp
Vice

Small pliers – side cutters
Small screwdrivers – flat and crosshead
Drill and selected drill bits
Small jeweller's saw
Small pair of scissors

This list will certainly handle the kit assemblies that I will cover later. Where specialised pieces of equipment are used, they will be suitably indicated.

CHAPTER 18
STOCK

I decided from the outset that my version of this layout will be the British Rail period when steam was still dominant. Locos were cleanish and the diesels of the green period were starting to come in. It doesn't really matter what anyone else thinks; you stock and run whatever takes your fancy. After all, it's your model railway!

The layout design with its hidden storage sidings will allow four complete trains to be stored, then a further train can be held in the terminus station platform. Furthermore, I decided that several trains from different regions would be seen together with one set of coaches served by two locos. This will result in an excess of motive power which can be held in the running shed on the upper level.

The siding below the retaining wall is there to hold a goods train (probably coal) that can do circuits round the lower level

then 'set back' into the siding. The other small siding can be used in two ways, one to hold a tank engine, say a Jinty 0–6–0, that can assist a train up the incline to the terminus once it has gone through the reverse loop. With the tunnel mouth set under the town, when the front of a loco is seen in the mouth, the rear of the train is clear of the main points so it could then 'set back' into one of the empty storage sidings. Secondly, it can be used to hold a mainline loco that has reversed down from the terminus and turned on the reverse loop before it returns to the upper level running shed. This movement eliminates the requirement for a turntable, which can be a very space-consuming accessory even if it looks impressive.

We have two isolation sections of track at the end of the two terminus roads, complete with uncoupling ramps, so, as the train enters the terminus, it stops, un-

A star in the locomotive department is this excellent model of a Britannia 4–6–2 *William Shakespeare* from Hornby.

A4 *Mallard* 4–6–2 is waiting to turn on the reverse loop and return to the top shed. Jinty 0–6–0 waits for a banking turn.

Other locos in the Hornby Railways range include 8F 2–8–0, Hunt class 4–4–0, 4–6–2 A3, 4–6–2 *Coronation Scot*, 0–4–0 saddle tank and 0–4–0 diesel shunter.

couples and then it can be isolated. Once the train departs, the loco can then be turned on the reverse lower loop and returned to the loco shed. Suggested stock so far includes an A4 *Mallard* with three Gresley coaches in blood and custard livery. Then there is a blood and custard rake of MK1 coaches with a Britannia and 2–10–0 9F locomotives. One of my favourites, perhaps a little out of period, is the maroon *Coronation Scot* streamlined 4–6–2 with period LMS rake. The platforms will accommodate a rake of three coaches and two locos. The *pièce de resistance* for me is the old

Tri-ang Blue Midland Pullman. This is a four-car set – two power units and two centre or parlor cars.

Making a Decision

With so much in the way of stock available, it can be difficult to make a decision on what sort of stock to run and what period actually to model. I include some selections of locos that are available from the major ready-to-run manufacturers. These are Hornby, Lima, Dapol, Mainline and

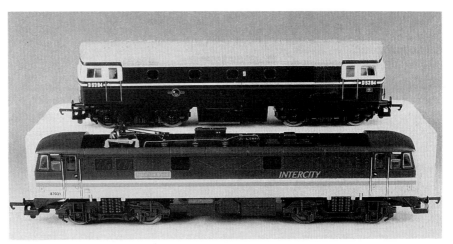

From the Lima range are these two, the Type 2 and a class 87 overhead electric in InterCity livery.

Bachmann. I haven't included rolling-stock, as it would take up too much space.

Because of the large plastic frogs on the Hornby points, the locos can sometimes stutter. This is due to the system used for electrical pick-up on the locos and tenders. Today's Hornby locos are wired in such a way that the tender picks up from one rail while the loco the other, thus giving the two polarities needed to power the motor. So, to help solve this problem, we can add extra pick-ups to the loco and tender. The more wheels you pick up from, the better the running will be, especially through the points, and as a bonus the slow running

will improve. The Tasma high frequency Relco unit will help in the general running as, when it contacts surface dirt on the track, it breaks it down through high frequency power.

As a model is taken out of the box it is bright, shiny and not too authentic, so a bit of careful weathering is needed to bring the loco to life. Again, it is not easy to show this in black and white; better in colour. So I can only advise that you look at old photos in some of the many full-size orientated magazines and books. Be careful, though, that the subject chosen is not a preserved item that has been lovingly res-

One of my prized trains is this old Tri-ang Blue Pullman.

tored to pristine condition rather like the one you've just taken out of the box – this is not authentic steam period condition.

In general, two basic colours are adequate for weathering if they are applied in different strengths. By this I mean how much thinners have been added to the base colour, so that, when it is sprayed, it doesn't swamp the detail. Washes of black can be applied around the smokebox, footplate, boiler top and cab roof; anywhere, in fact, that soot and dust is likely to settle. Rust colour should be applied to the lower mechanisms, such as valve gear, wheels, brakes and axleboxes on the tender; also, areas that are worn such as steps and handrails. The latter is best dry-brushed, and this technique can also be used to highlight detail such as rivets, pipes etc. To dry-brush, take a brush and cover it with paint, then wipe it dry on a suitable cloth or tissue until almost dry then carefully flick the bristles across the detail. Paint will be deposited on this detail but only highlighting it. The degree of highlighting is determined by how much paint is applied, ie the number of coats.

Another area where a degree of individualism can be achieved is by adding further details to your locos and, of course, stock. For details, such as lamps, crew, vacuum pipes, brakes where required, tools such as shovels, oil cans – in fact all the sort of items usually seen on a loco – again study photos. To take detailing one stage further, Crownline from Cornwall offer an enormous range of detailing kits suitable for a very wide selection of ready-to-run locos. They range from simple detailing kits to almost complete rebuilds.

CHAPTER 19
WHITE METAL KITS

There are two ways that a white metal kit can be put together. The first is to use a two-part epoxy resin, where equal parts are squeezed from each tube, mixed together and carefully put on the parts that will be joined together. The drawback here, of course, is the time required for the glue to dry at each stage of construction, making building very slow and time-consuming. The second method, and certainly much more acceptable once the technique has been mastered, is soldering, Using this method, construction is both quick and very strong. Now, if an error is made during soldering, and the parts are

not damaged, then they can be unsoldered and the error adjusted. With gluing, of course, the whole thing is a lot different and more difficult.

As I know from talking to many modellers, there are substantial fears of soldering white metal kits together. However, Hubert Carr, of Carr's Modelling Products, has recently made available the ideal soldering iron suited purely for white metal kit construction. Naturally, the correct solder and relevant fluxes are also available through Carr's. As with any form of modelling, nothing will replace practice. This will, in turn, inspire confi-

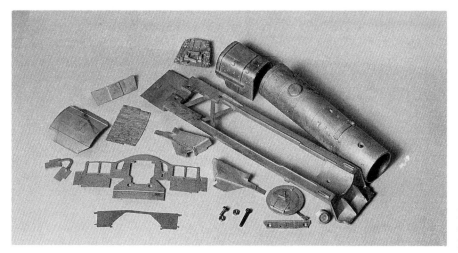

Basic white metal castings and etched brass pieces for the loco body.

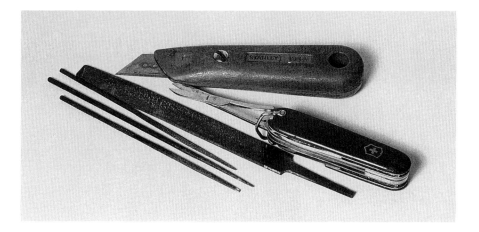

Basic tools include files, knife and scissors.

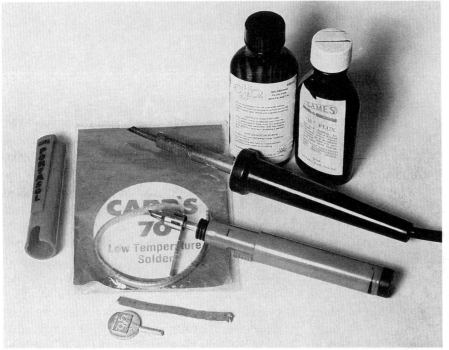

Soldering requires a low-temperature iron and solder and flux, some examples of which are shown.

dence, which will make the whole thing a lot easier as time goes on. So get stuck in and you'll find within a short space of time it will be second nature.

Apart from the correct iron and solder and flux, the next most important thing is the cleanliness of the parts being joined together. A fibre pen or stick will clean away the oxide layer, leaving good clean metal ready to take solder. If a joint is clean and well fluxed, then, when the soldering iron is loaded with a small amount

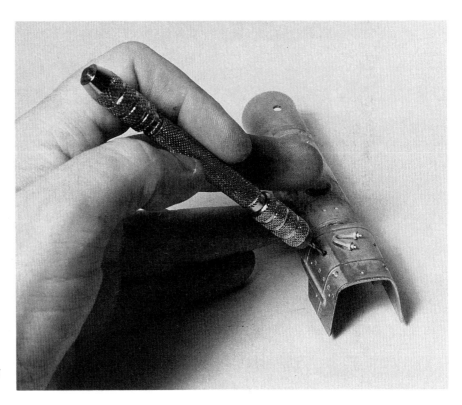

A pin-chuck is used to drill out the washout plug holes.

A home-made bending bar in a clamp is used to form the cab.

Etched cab, cast firebox and boiler on the footplate.

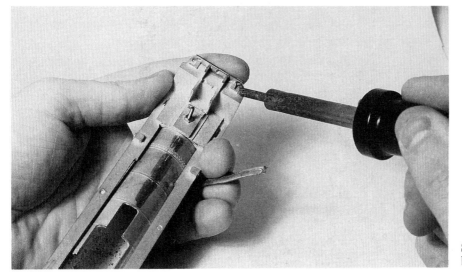

Soldering the front buffer beam onto the footplate.

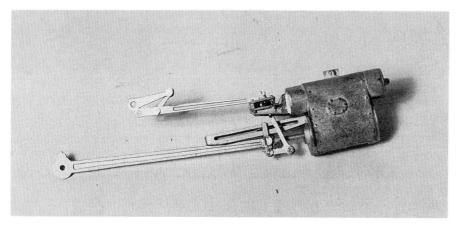

Care should be taken when putting together the valve gear.

The chassis minus the motor.

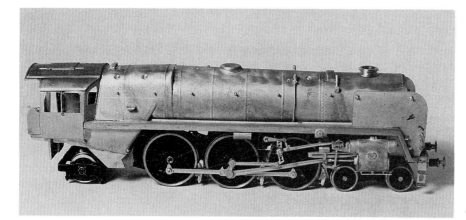

The loco prior to painting.

of solder and is brought to the joint, you will see it run up or down the seam like a silver line. When that happens every time, your soldering is becoming proficient. Remember when putting white metal kits together, or etched brass kits come to that, to hold the bits to be soldered together correctly and comfortably. You'll know when

it's wrong, as you may smell burning flesh and it will hurt! The subject for the kit build is the DJH 4mm scale BR standard 4–6–2 Britannia locomotive and tender. This range of kits is superbly detailed and, what's more important, go together very well.

CHAPTER 20
BUILDING 'O' GAUGE 'ELECTRICS'

While the old LNWR has been my interest for a number of years, a change of scale from P4 to 7mm also coincided with a change in period. While still remaining loyal to the Premier Line, my models now represent the current 25Kv electric locos seen in and around Euston Station.

The kits are from the RJH Model Railways range, with a good degree of modification and extra detailing. Each loco was correct at the time it was photographed and, while there are constant updates and minor changes in both detail and livery on the prototype, I've kept them as initially seen.

Bogie Power

I have now standardised on two motors per engine and these are RG7 Portescap motor/gearbox units. They are expensive, and aren't getting any cheaper as time goes on, and may in due course cause a rethink of this situation. Why the RG7 over the standard RJH motor and gears?

While taking nothing away from the latter, RG7 units are the most powerful and ideally suitable for their kits, particularly when used in pairs and combined with the Delrin chain drive, which I have also fitted to each loco bogie thus giving them 4-axle drive as opposed to 4wd. Because the RG7 units are designed with larger diameter driving wheels in mind, more usually associated with steam outline models, the gearing is such that maximum speed of my electric locos only relates to around 70 mph. This ensures that even the most exuberant operator can't cause too much of a high speed crash. It also makes them very controllable at lower speeds and, of course, very powerful. When tested on the old Cromerford and High Peak layout, the class 85 loco managed to do one circuit of the layout, a scale mile, with 19 heavy scratchbuilt coaches behind it with only minimal slipping; this is certainly adequate for most loco pulling requirements.

In order to fit the RG7 into the standard loco etched chassis, cut a square hole into the motormount end big enough to clear

Class 90 No 90 046 in 'double diamond' triple grey Railfreight livery which carries Fox Transfers, prototype transfer in this scale.

Class 85 No 85 109 is in the original blue livery. The long service this class of loco has endured has been portrayed with heavy weathering and worn paint. Even the screen shows the path of the wipers.

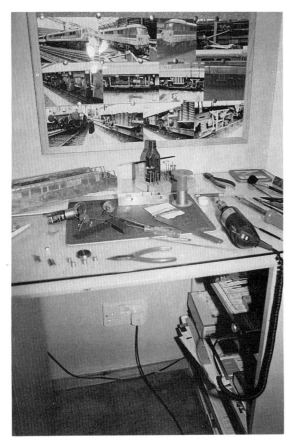

For each project have a good selection of prototype pictures to work from. Use a peg board.

the gearbox when offered centrally over the axle. And, in order to accommodate the Delrin chain drive system, the sprockets need to have their shanks shortened and two small vees cut into the resulting shank, so that superglue can be added at a later date to lock them on the axle. Also, you need to cut the brass top hat bearing away inside to clear the gearbox and sprocket when on the axle side by side.

Motor Bogie

While wheel centres are given for most of the classes, always check against the bogie side frames. Mark off where the ends of the sideframes will couple to the end cross-braces that run across the ends of the etched chassis. A nice touch, mainly cosmetic, is to remove a triangle of brass from each bottom corner of the etched chassis so that, when the completed bogie is viewed from the side, a horrible square lump is not visible at each end.

I prefer to spray the etched chassis black once they are finished, minus the wheels, and at the same time, but separately, the completed side frames after they have

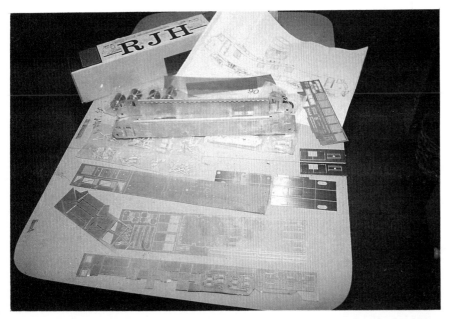

The brass etches that are included with the RJH kits. This one is for a class 90.

been thoroughly washed and dried. For this I use a product made by Spectra called Sprayclean which is an excellent cleaner that removes finger grease, stains, etc. prior to spraying paint on the subject. For painting, use an ordinary aerosol spray can of matt black and hold the subjects for spraying with surgical forceps. This cuts down the 'black finger nail' syndrome.

The most vulnerable items on the sideframes are the etched brass steps which are reasonably fragile anyway but, when hung on the side of a large white metal casting, they manage to get knocked by all sorts of things. I therefore add additional strengtheners to the bottom of the steps, in the form of a U-shaped piece of brass wire which is soldered to the lower step and then into additionally drilled holes in the sideframe. Before spraying the black, put a spot of Humbrol Maskol onto the inside of the sideframe ends where they will join the cross pieces, and the outer ends of the bogie cross pieces. Then remove this masking after spraying. The masking will also help when soldering these items together later, as the metal surfaces will be clean.

Finally on the bogie, the wheels. Those supplied in the kit have a small nylon bush at one end to insulate the axle, necessary for two rail running. Unfortunately, the brass top hat bearing manages to bridge this gap and causes a short. To overcome this, I fit large discs cut from clear plastic to the insulated wheel side which just fits over the axles giving good insulation. When assembling the bogies remember the following points:

Bogies will be different polarities, and will face outwards with motors innermost, so get insulated axles on opposite sides.
Note position of Delrin chain and slots in chassis spacers.
Lightly superglue threaded wheels onto axles.
Solder on sideframes with steps at the front making sure they are central both vertically and horizontally.

Once all the above is correct, attach wires and couple up to a chocolate block, place on a test-track and watch them go in opposite directions – very frustrating. If this happens, swap the motor wires round on one bogie.

Roof Pan

RJH loco kits are designed with the body being pre-formed into a U-shape, complete with the top of the sides turned-in for the class 81/85/86/87 and 90s. The class 89 is designed differently but, as it is a one-off

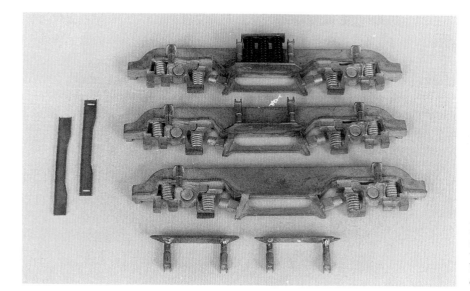

Building up the sideframes with the various castings, shocks, body springs and etched cross pieces.

prototype, we'll not worry about it here. To complete the square, the roof pan is dropped in along with the white metal cab roof castings. So, we start construction with the roof pan.

The first hurdle to cross is the bending of the short sides that go the full length of the pan. For this, clamp a large piece of ½in square steel, which is say 12 in long, and secure at both ends with small clamps to a piece of wood, placing the piece of steel close to the inside of the fold line. Then, with a ruler or large file, gently bend the sides up moving along the complete length. End up by gently tapping the now right-angled side with a small hammer, so removing any small kinks. Repeat the same procedure with the other side.

Next is the preparation of the roof fittings, both white metal and lost wax brass castings. Drill out the holes in the pan to take the various castings, and clean all the mould lines from them, then solder in the brass ones first. These are the insulators for the Pantagraph with 4-core solder and the white metal castings with low melt solder, and I strongly recommend the use of solder, rather than glue, with these kits. I use an Orynx 100 watt soldering iron that gets a lot of heat into the job and, with care and technique, you can use the one iron for soldering all types of metal, brass down to white metal alike. The key word is 'heat' – do it and remove it quickly. When using 4-core solder, put the solder onto the tip and take it to the job in

The complete motor bogie, ready painted black with gears and Delrin chain drive in place.

These are the bogie steps
which need reinforcing.

question. With white metal, never touch
the iron onto the castings and, when fixing
them to brass, always tin the brass first
with low melt solder, put in the casting,
add flux and then put the iron onto the
metal (not the casting) which will then
transfer the heat, melt the low melt solder
and fix the casting in position.

When soldering parts, think out the
order they will be put together in terms of
the amount of heat needed to join them
together. Start with brass to brass, then
thin brass to brass such as overlays and
finish off with white metal to brass. That
way, if you think out the order, you reduce
the risk of damaging a soft casting by
using too much heat on another soldering
operation that requires more heat.

Sub-Units

In order to help in the construction of these
electric locos, I find it best to build up as
many sub-units as possible so that the
final construction will be quick as the loco
takes shape.

With this in mind, build up the under-
floor mounted units. These are combinations of etched brass braces and white metal
castings. Once they are built, clean up and
put to one side until all the units are
complete. The next items are the white
metal roofs. It will need some work on the
body to ensure a good fit. Hold the roofs in
position with large rubber bands and
tweak the brass body until you're sure all
is square. Once this is done, solder

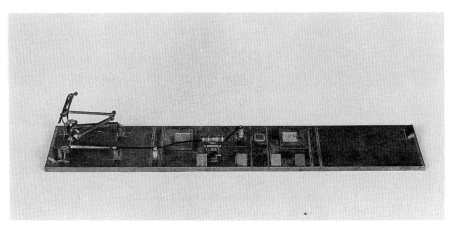

The roof pan with roof
fittings, both white metal,
and lost wax brass fitted.

Fit the roof pan and then make sure the cab roof fits the cab sides.

together the various body sections, such as the buffer beams, cab backhead, floor, cab front, and cab instrument panels.

Body Reinforcement

In order to maintain the squareness of the body box, and at the same time add some strength, glue lengths of 3 or 4 mm thick ply to the sides inside the body, allowing for the window apertures, etc. Also add interior bulkheads, three will do. These will stop the body being squeezed in when being handled after it is finished, as then it becomes a nightmare to try to correct.

Add slots in the bulkheads at the top so that the bogie motor wires can be threaded through, when they are fixed in.

Refinements

All of my locos are fitted with flexible hoses with lost wax brass fittings for the air pipes and the cables. I also like the sprung buffers to be reasonably soft, so that when the loco buffers up to a train, they compress realistically. I have added radio telephone aerials to the roof, including the conduit taking the wires down to the cab. A casting for the radio telephone

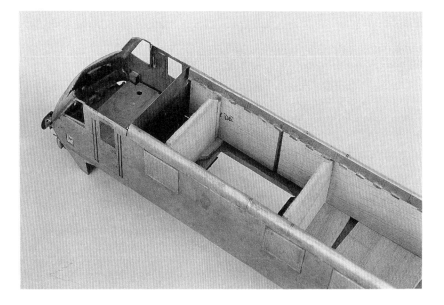

Inside the body, fit pieces of ply and additional bulk heads to give strength.

The various lower sub-units are built up and cleaned before construction of the body.

is available from David Parkin's Modern Motive Power range, and includes a separate telephone hand set.

Painting

The key to a successful paint job lies in a well-prepared loco body after you have finished building. To this end, always shotblast the model after you've finished construction. This not only gives a superb surface finish onto which you can apply the paint, but it also removes a lot of the solder and muck that tends to build up in all the nooks and crannies. Removal of this muck helps the model to regain its sharpness, and enhances any of the detail that may have been covered or filled in during soldering.

First apply a good primer, preferably to a warm model. Use ordinary car aerosol primer available from most DIY centres.

Use 'Railmatch' paints, produced by Howes of Oxford, which are excellent, both in colour strength and covering. The code numbers of paints in the range match those numbers on the official BR painting diagrams, a very useful and thoughtful refinement.

For the various liveries, some of which use up to six different colours, reverse masking is the best way of building up the different liveries. This method requires paint being applied, allowing it to dry and then masking it off so that the next coat can then be applied. 3M car lining tape is superb for parallel lines down the sides of the bodies, which must be perfect, as in this scale any error is big and will be easily noticed.

It is best to spray the yellow first, then move up the lighter colours through to the darkest finishing with black and, once all the paint is dry, apply the transfers and varnish the whole thing. For the latter,

The completed loco in brass state prior to cleaning and then painting.

Floquil is available from Victor's in Pentonville Road, London. Mix gloss and flat to give a nice sheen finish, then allow several days for it all to dry thoroughly.

Glazing

The cab roofs are made removable so that, after painting, the cab windows can be glazed. Use the material provided, but cut out each window separately, then apply it with small drops of superglue to hold it in position. Finish up by applying a good wedge of 5-minute, two-part epoxy resin to all four sides of each window. This overkill of securing the windows will help to ensure that they survive several inquisitive prods by those infuriating people who have to touch the windows. It's extremely difficult to refit a window once someone has kindly pushed it in, so make it strong to start with.

After the glazing, add the flexible pipes, nameplates, silver arrows or swallows as required. Then fit the power bogies, wire-up and place it on shed with the others.

CHAPTER 21
PAINTING AND LINING

The airbrush has always been an important instrument for the graphic artist and, with modern production methods and techniques, it has become a relatively cheap tool for the model maker.

Since the early part of this century when the airbrush was first invented, it has been developed to a degree which would astonish those early pioneers. There are brushes now available which are capable of producing some of the most complex and versatile work and, while we are concerned mainly with projecting paint at model railway equipment, if you obtain, for instance, the Badger airbrush catalogue, you will see just what can be done with some of the more sophisticated brushes.

Basically there are two different types of airbrush: external mix and internal mix. External mix brushes mix the air and paint outside the head, and produce a slightly coarser spray pattern, while internal mix brushes produce a smoother pattern, mixing the air and paint inside the spraying head. The internal mix brushes can also be sub-divided into single and dual action. This refers to the trigger action of the airbrush. 'Single action' is the method which triggers the amount of air being drawn through the brush, the amount of paint having already been set by a screw at the end of the handle controlling the position of the needle. 'Dual action' brushes have only one control for paint and air. The trigger on top of the brush has a dual movement, being pressed down for air, and then pulled back for paint. This type of brush is obviously the most sophisticated type and, of course, the most expensive. Thus, with this type of brush, one action controls the amount of both air and paint and, with a little practice, the most finest of work can be obtained.

Now, which brush should you choose when looking at all the different types and makes on the market? Over the past few years, I have tried various types of brushes by different manufacturers and have found that they all perform very well, within the different designs and uses for which they are intended. The cheapest brush on the market is that sold by Humbrol, which

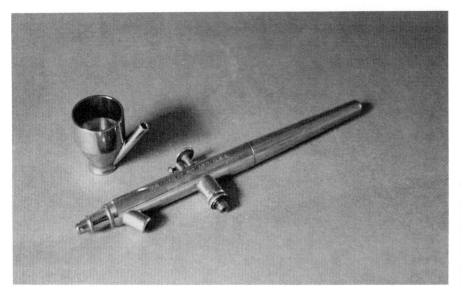

The most important single item for good quality painting is a decent airbrush. Morris and Ingram (London) Ltd (address in Appendix A) are Badger airbrush importers.

retails at around £15, depending on where you buy it. It is fairly crude and basically blows air across a tube in a jar full of thinned paint. This results in a very wide spray pattern and wastes quite a lot of paint but, if care is taken, good results will be obtained.

Next up the scale of sophistication and price is the single action outside admission tube, ie the Badger 350 and Paache 'H'. The Paache is very good and costs in the region of £50. The Badger is of a very similar design but is not quite as robust as the Paache. Both brushes can be adapted from spraying light links and water colours to heavier enamels and high viscosity materials, simply by changing needle and valve cone assemblies. The Badger 350 costs approximately £50. In the ranges of airbrushes easily available, only Badger, so far as I know, provide the single action internal mix type, with their model 200. At a current price of approximately £65, this is understandably a very popular brush amongst modellers and with practice will give similar results to the Badger 100, 150 Paache V and VL double action brushes. Both of these types have interchangeable head and needle assemblies to spray light materials in lines $\frac{1}{16}''$ wide to heavier fluids such as cellulose paints, acrylics and ceramic glazes.

Generally, airbrushes by different manufacturers are pretty much the same in operation, and really it comes down to what you can afford to pay. I am firmly of the opinion that, when buying tools of any description, you should go for quality and it is worth paying that little bit extra for it. As I said, the Paache 'H' is a reasonably good brush with single action and external mix. With its interchangeable head assemblies, it will cope with most spraying jobs and is extremely easy to maintain and keep clean. However, what it gains in easy maintenance, it loses in its spray pattern, which is of a large dot or coarse pattern.

Of the internal mix brushes, the Badger 200 is as good as you will find, and gains on the Paache with its small dot finer spray pattern. More care, however, is needed maintenance-wise, because the paint and air are mixed inside the body of the brush. Recently I have been using the Badger 150, together with its own compressor. I have found that the cost involved, £100 for the brush and £85 for the compressor, represent good value for money.

Now that we have established that the airbrush is a good tool for us, how do we make use of it and what do we use to get the paint from its container on to the model? Basically, there are four ways of

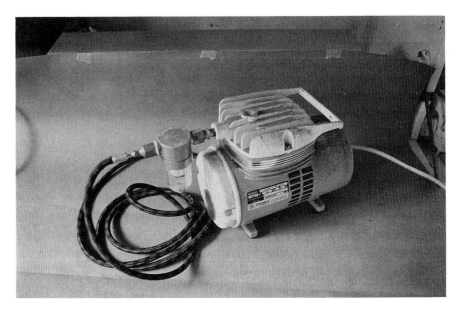

The second most important item is a decent compressor, again from Morris and Ingram.

propelling the paint in the direction we want it. The two most common are pressurised propellant cans sold by most, if not all, of the airbrush manufacturers, and compressed air from small compressors, again supplied by the brush manufacturers. All the suppliers also provide an adaptor to fit the airbrush line to a car tyre, but don't use the spare from your car, as constant inflation and deflation can damage the tyre. However, a rim and tyre from a local scrap merchant will provide clean propulsion, if a little cumbersome. The fourth option we have is a CO_2 gas cylinder. These are good if you do a lot of spraying and you find the noise of the compressor a nuisance. However, the cylinders are very heavy and difficult to move about. The initial financial outlay is fairly excessive and, of course, some sort of regulator is also required. By the time cylinder rental has been taken into account, this is probably at least halfway towards the cost of a small compressor.

The best two options for us are the propellant cans or a small compressor. The cans come in various sizes and will suffice for those who will use the airbrush two or three times a year. A word of warning here, though – the propellant can run out at the most inappropriate moment, so, if a paint job is about to be started, always make sure there is sufficient propellant to finish the job. For the modeller who sprays a number of models a year, a compressor becomes an absolute boon and will soon pay for itself, not only in monetary terms if you have been buying lots of propellant cans, but in sheer convenience of use. With the airbrush linked up to your propellant, now comes the moment when you press the trigger and air comes through the brush for the first time. Before trying to spray any paint, add some thinners, or even cold water, to the cup or bottle and experiment with the brush characteristics. If possible, hold the brush at arm's length in the light and spray at right angles to your line of sight. By moving the needle or nozzle back and forth, you will get a good idea of the spray pattern of your brush.

Before any serious experiments are carried out, however, I would strongly recommend that you wear a mask of some sort, covering nose and mouth. Quite a simple affair is all that is needed – the industrial kind, using a gauze filter and metal holder, is perfectly adequate, and available at very reasonable cost from DIY shops. This is to prevent any droplets of thinners and paint entering the nose and throat, as any of the paint solvents can be toxic if sufficient quantities are ingested.

Paint

What type of paint should be used with an airbrush? For the modeller, the two most popular ranges of paint available are Humbrol and Precision. Both market a large range of colours in specialist modelling areas, and Humbrol in particular offer a good range of more general colours in both gloss and matt finishes. Both ranges are oil-based enamel paints, available from just about all the model railway and general modelling shops throughout the UK, and can be thinned either with their own brand name thinners or white spirit, or even pure turpentine.

As a paint for general use, I have always found that Humbrol takes a lot of beating and in the past few years has improved considerably, after what seemed to be a period where paint quality seemed inconsistent. Some of their colours still seem to be a little 'muddy', however, and this is where Precision score with their range of railway colours. Covering power though, does sometimes leave something to be desired, but I will cover this later in this chapter.

Other oil-based paints are supplied by DBI and Compucolour and seem to be similar in character to Humbrol and Precision. Another paint available for our use is Floquil, imported from the USA by Victors. Floquil is not oil-based, nor is it based on cellulose. Its base is an industrial solvent – Xylene – which, although distilled from oil, has a subtle difference which, not

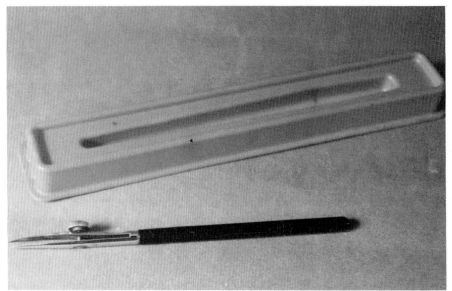

A decent quality bow pen
is needed for fine lining.

being a chemist, I cannot quantify. I can say, however, that as a paint, Floquil is probably the best paint for small-scale models available in this country. Covering capacity is excellent and, currently at £1.80 per 1 fl oz bottle, represents very good value for money. It has one drawback in that the colours are formulated for American modellers, but their Engine Black and varnishes particularly are worth looking at. There are, of course, many other paints available for use on our models, such as cellulose, acrylics, water colours, poster paints, gouache, etc. but, as we are mostly concerned at the moment with rolling-stock, the mention of these will suffice.

We need, more often than not, to thin down our paints with their respective thinners for spraying and I prefer to do this in separate airtight jars, transferring the paint at the right consistency to the airbrush cup or bottle. In this way, paint is not wasted, and can be kept in storage ready to spray when the next job in that colour comes along. It is difficult to give a definitive answer to how much paint should be thinned. Some makes need more than others, indeed some colours from the same range of paints differ in the amount of thinning needed. Suffice it to say that the consistency should be like pouring cream. Not as thin as milk, but thinner than double cream.

Start by stirring your tin of paint thoroughly. 'Thoroughly' means stirring with some sort of broad-based implement, such as a lolly stick, for about four to five

A paint handle such as this from Railway lines (see Appendix A for address), can hold loco bodies during painting.

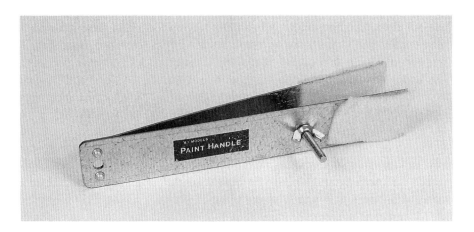

minutes. This is more important with matt paints as, if all the matting agent is not mixed in, a streaky finish could result. Once this has been done, pour about one third of the tinlet (assuming Humbrol or Precision), into your mixing jar. With an eye dropper, add to the paint approximately half that amount in thinners. Put on the cap and shake well to mix the two together, and then have a look at the result. In general, if the thinned paint has covered the inside of the lid and does not run away, the consistency is about right. However, it is now worth trying your airbrush with actual paint and, should the spraying consistency be wrong, this can be adjusted as you go along. A small amount of the thinned paint should be transferred to your airbrush cup or bottle. I prefer using a side cup or bottle, not only because it is easy to keep clean, but less paint is wasted.

The main object in using your airbrush for the first time is to get the 'feel' of the brush, and the best way of doing this is to find the minimum and maximum lines that the brush can provide by spraying white or light coloured card pinned at about shoulder height to a vertical surface. Depending on the type of brush you have chosen, try varying the air pressure through the trigger, and generally explore the characteristics inherent in the brush. Always keep the brush moving and start to spray just before hitting the card. Keep the brush moving parallel with the card, and stop spraying when the jet of paint has passed the edge of the card. In this way you will get used to using the brush and it will also give you an idea of your own skill. At the same time you will be able to experiment with the consistency of the paint and get to know better whether you have mixed it too thin or too thick. It is a simple matter to add either paint or thinners to the mix until it is just right. If it is too thick, it will be drying as it comes out of the nozzle of the brush, and will create a fuzzy effect on the card. If it is too thin, it will start to run before covering the card. At this time, once the general characteristics have been mastered, try painting an old plastic wagon body to get an idea of what a model is going to look like when it has been sprayed.

Of course, once you have used paint through your airbrush, it needs to be cleaned, and this seems to be one area that puts many people off using airbrushes. When demonstrating at exhibitions, one question which keeps cropping up is, "yes, that's all very well, but how do you keep it clean?". The basic rule here is to clean the

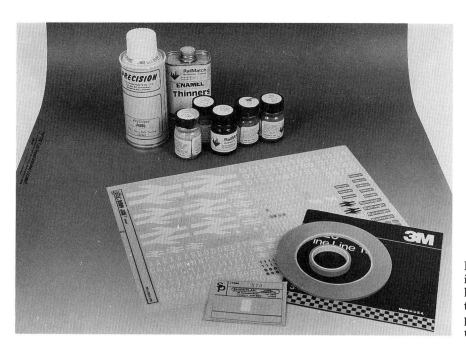

For painting electric locos in the modern image liveries, these are some of the paints, transfers, plates and lining tapes used.

brush as soon as you have finished using it. The first thing is to clean your jar or cup. Any paint left in these should be poured back into the mixing jar, and then they should be rinsed out with thinners. Once this has been done, spray some neat thinners through the gun until no trace of paint is left. Withdraw the needle and, with a cotton bud dipped into the thinners, clean the nozzle so that any build-up of paint is cleaned away. That, really, is it, and, once you get into the habit, it will become second nature. Periodically, perhaps, when each model is completed, refer to your instruction book and remove the needle and nozzle assembly, and gently clean all the surfaces with another cotton bud and thinners.

With the practice you will get by experimenting in this way, you will gain confidence and feel able to paint those kits that you have hesitated to spray, as you feel that a bad job will spoil your model. Have confidence and, if you proceed step by step, with patience you will never want to consider brush painting anything ever again.

Brushes do, of course, have their uses and we will be discussing these later.

However, now that we have the means, let us go on and describe the stages in painting an actual model.

Preparation

Naturally, the model must be clean, dry and free of grease and dirt, or anything that will detract from a good paint finish. To achieve this, it is important to have as many sub-assemblies as possible, with, say, bogie and/or pony trucks removed, for instance, from the chassis. Any solvent is good for degreasing – carbon tetra-chloride, xylene, MEK, etc. Mek-Pak and Peco Electroclean are easily available from model shops. After a wash with one of these, the model should then be given a good scrub with some sort of household cleaner, Ajax, Vim or similar, using an old soft toothbrush, or ½″ paintbrush, given a good rinse and left to dry in a dust-free atmosphere. I keep a strong cardboard box for this, and then place it in the airing cupboard overnight. This thoroughly warms the model, and this is important as we come on to the next stage.

A simple spray booth can be built using a cabinet and fitting a flexible hose to an extracter fan. The cake stand is ideal for putting models on during spraying.

Priming

I once went to pick up some paint from a local garage and, while waiting for it, watched through the window a car being resprayed. What intrigued me was that the sides of the car were being heated, quite strongly, within infra-red heaters. After about five minutes, they were moved away by the sprayer's assistant, and more or less immediately, a coat of cellulose primer was applied to the bare metal. This puzzled me for some time, but the thought occurred to me that it had been done for some reason, so I applied a similar method when priming models. It wasn't until a couple of years later I was told that it is done to exclude water vapour. The warmer the surface, the more water vapour is excluded, and therefore the primer will stick that much better. QED. By putting your model into the airing cupboard overnight, you are, in fact, reproducing this effect and therefore should get the first coat of primer onto the model without delay.

For priming the model, I have found that there is nothing better than aerosol cans of cellulose primer from your local garage or car accessory shop. There are two colours, grey and red oxide, and I find that I use either of these more or less exclusively, mostly because of convenience and the cost – approximately £1.00.

As with any painting job, it is important that thin and even coats are applied. It is far better to put a thin coat on, allow to dry and then put on another, rather than trying to save time by spraying a thick coat and then watching the paint or primer running and completely spoiling the model.

Painting

Earlier I mentioned that the covering power of some of the modelling paints left something to be desired, and this is particularly true of red, be it Midland, LMS Maroon, etc. This is where I always use the red oxide primer, to give a much richer feel to the top coat. This method can also be used in providing a 'background' colour for any of the top coats which appear to be a little 'thin'. By using the grey primer and then an undercoat, the top coat will cover so much better. This method is exactly the same as that when painting new woodwork in the house – primer, undercoat, topcoat.

Apart from problems associated with covering power, once you have become practiced and proficient with your airbrush, it will be second nature to use it as much as possible. However, this is not to say that your ordinary brush will become redundant because it will not. On small-scale models, it is easier to spray the main body colour, assuming that there is more than one, and then brush paint the smokebox, footplate, etc.

To avoid brush marks in the paint, good quality brushes are essential, and again it involves paying that little bit extra for quality tools. There are many small paint-brushes about in various model shops, but to find the best it is worth visiting a good artists' shop where they will have on display a range of the better quality brushes available. I always use Winsor & Newton's best sables, of which there are a number of different ranges. Their Series 16 artist's sables are good for general purpose work, in sizes from 0–3, and for a good miniature sable I choose the series 12, available from 000 upwards. Caring for these brushes is important too, costing as they do from approximately £2 for the 000 size. I always keep two bottles of thinners for brush cleaning, one to take out as much paint as possible and the other, which I change frequently to keep it as clean as possible, for final rinsing. In addition, if you do a lot of painting with your brushes, it is worth washing them fairly frequently with soap and warm water. It is sometimes astonishing the paint that is left on what looks like a clean brush.

As yet, I have not mentioned the small aerosol spray cans available from both Humbrol and Precision. There are now a large number of these available, with paint quality matching exactly that in the small tinlets, but ready-mixed for spraying. All that is necessary is to give the cans a vigorous shake for about two minutes and they are ready to use. In their way, they are perfectly adequate for what they are intended to do, but are very wasteful of paint, and, of course, there can be no adjustment whatsoever of the paint flow.

Lining

Lining – quite an emotive word in the model railway field, but with thought, a good bow pen and a fairly steady hand, you will be able to achieve good constant width lines that, with practice, you will be very pleased with.

The first piece of equipment we need for making these lines is, as I said, a good quality bow pen. Mine have fairly long thin blades, which taper down to a fairly sharp point. They should not be so sharp, however, that the blade points score the paint as they are drawn across the surface. They should be easy to adjust with a knurled knob, to mate properly when screwed together. The inside faces too must be absolutely flat, otherwise no paint will flow. I have used the same type of pen now for about 10 years, replacing it when it becomes worn. I have worn out two so far, but depending on how much you use your pen, it should last a lifetime. My pen is manufactured by Kern in Switzerland, Pattern No. 1039, imported into this country by Letraset and costs between £20 and £25.

Practice is needed to achieve consistently fine lines, but, like the airbrush, with patience and confidence it is possible. To start, paint a piece of plastic card, about 6in × 3in with the main body colour, and allow the paint to dry (about 8 hours to be safe).

To digress, I always use matt colours wherever possible as they dry fairly quickly and are 'handleable' in just a few minutes.

For consistent lining, new tins of paint are essential for every model as, once a tin has been opened to the atmosphere, the pigment (colour) carrier will start to evaporate and the paint thicken up. To achieve a straight line, some sort of straight edge is necessary, and for most work I use a 12in plastic ruler cut down to about 7in long. This length is adequate without being unwieldy for 99% of all lining work, and being plastic will not damage paintwork when the ruler is rested on the model. The plastic surface, too, is similar to a painted surface and the bow pen can be tried and adjusted before starting to line on the model.

However, back to practising on our piece of plastic card. The bow pen should be adjusted so that a gap of approximately 1–2mm is left at the tips. A small amount of paint is then dropped into the gap. I use a small jeweller's screwdriver and the gap closed on the tips. The paint will be drawn down to the tips by capillary action, and should then be drawn across the plastic card. With a little perseverance, you will find that it won't be long before you are able to draw consistent thin lines.

My general method of lining is to line as much as possible directly onto the model. However, some transfers are needed, normally just boiler bands, but in this case, the splashers will need to be lined in this way, as they are obscured by various pipes and fittings, etc., on the footplate.

To manufacture 'in house' transfers is fairly simple and involves spraying some waterslide transfer paper with body colour and drawing out the transfers you need. Plain waterslide transfer paper is sometimes difficult to get hold of and may also need to be varnished to provide the actual carrier film. However, any sheet of ready-made waterslide transfers will provide what we want.

I have sprayed half a sheet of Kemco lining with body colour, only because this was the cheapest sheet available in my local model shop. Any sheet of waterslide transfers will do, even those for aircraft or ships, as we are covering them up anyway. I draw out straight lines for the boiler bands and the full lining for each splasher.

While spraying the base coat on the loco, overspray a piece of transfer sheet.

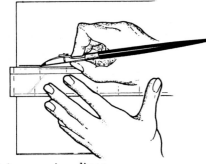

Rule on various lines.

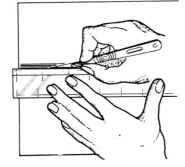

Finally, cut lining with a scalpel ready to be applied to loco.

By using the draughtsman's curves, a curved line to the correct radius is drawn in first and, by measuring the depth of the splasher, the straight line is then drawn in at the correct distance from the top of the curved line. If the correct radius cannot be found on the draughtsman's curves, dividers can be used to cut a circle from some 30 thou plastic card, and this is then used to provide the correct radius.

As I have already said, most of the lining must go straight onto the model and this is where your practice on the piece of plastic card comes in. By applying the same technique as lining the plastic card, some of the more simple lines on the model should now be tackled. The tender is nice and straightforward to start off with. Now, by loading the pen with some paint, a panel about 2mm wide is drawn around the complete tender side. This will be dry in a few minutes and the exercise repeated on the other side and back of the tender. While this is drying, the locomotive should be tackled. Start with the cab sides and then the footplate. Any curves can be either put in with an 000 brush, or alternatively, a plastic card template can be cut to the correct radius, and drawn round with the pen.

It is best to leave the lining for two or three hours to harden properly. When this is done, most of the main lining is complete, and the rest of the minor lining can be undertaken. Approach it in a step-by-step manner, edging everything in black first, using the pen and ruler as much as possible, or cutting small pieces of plastic card, held in place with the end of a craft knife, where the ruler would be too far away from the model. Use an 000 brush slightly dampened with thinners to put in the smaller curves. You will, perhaps, have noticed that I do not support the model or ruler in any way when lining, preferring to lay the ruler on the model surface. This is not to say that you shouldn't. Some modellers like to do this when they are lining, propping up the model so it does not wobble about. The ruler is then supported either side on some books or similar and the lining carried out.

I have also not mentioned the use of modern draughtsman's pens, ie Rotring, Staedler, etc. Until very recently, none of the inks, except black, intended for these pens have been of much use, as they are nowhere near dense enough and intended for use on paper and card. The use of the black ink can be recommended, though, and I have found nib sizes giving a line width of 0.25mm and 0.5mm to be useful. If you do use one of these, however, be careful of getting any thinners or methylated spirit onto the ink, as it will smudge badly. Just on the market is a range of acrylic paints by Winsor & Newton, which although a little thin for use in a bow pen, will not clog up these draughtsman's technical pens. The range is called Designers Brilliant Watercolours.

At this stage, with all the lining in place, with the exception of the homemade transfer for the boiler bands and splashers, I give the whole model a thin coat of eggshell varnish, of which more later. No transfers like to stick to matt surfaces, so a coat of varnish will help here.

Transfer

In the main, we have four types of ready printed transfers available: Methfix, Pressfix, Waterslide and Rub Down. Methfix and Pressfix are a huge range of numbers, lettering and lining transfers from PC Models, for virtually every railway company pre- and post-grouping. Some are neglected, unfortunately for I have my own particular favourites: GNR, NER and GER.

Methfix: This type of transfer has an inert gum as an adhesive which will react with methylated spirits to stick to the model. Each letter or number should be cut from the transfer sheet with a sharp knife, and with the appropriate transfer in the correct place, well wetted with a solution of 3:1 meths and water and then pressed into place. After about five minutes, the backing paper can be soaked off with cold water and any excess gum washed away.

Pressfix On a similar backing sheet to the Methfix type, Pressfix transfers are intended to be, as the name implies, pressed into place. Instead of the gum of Methfix, they carry an adhesive which holds the transfer in place. After a time, this adhesive may dry up, but can be revived by spraying some mounting adhesive onto the back of the transfer sheet. Once in place, each number or figure should be rubbed with a ball point or similar, and the backing paper soaked off.

In positioning transfers on a model, it is very noticeable if one character is even

0.5mm out of position. To avoid this, I always cut out the letter or number with a sharp knife and metal rule, endeavouring to cut as close to the character as possible, particularly at the top and bottom. After positioning on the model with the rule and the backing paper removed, the characters will all be in line.

Waterslide For some reason, this type of transfer has never been very popular with railway modellers, but aircraft and ship modellers use very little else. By soaking each character in water, it is slid off the backing paper and into place on the model. With boiler bands, however, it is easier to push the complete transfer behind pipes and handrails, etc, wetted well with a fairly large brush and then, after removing the backing paper, slid into place. To cover up any carrier film, the transfers should be applied onto a gloss surface.

Rub Down Type Better known to most people as Letraset type, the transfer is positioned over the correct place on the model and then rubbed down, through the clear carrier, onto the model. Not a very easy type to use, they are intended more for use on paper and card. I much prefer using the Methfix type, even though the excess gum is sometimes difficult to remove.

Varnishes

It is worth experimenting with the different varnishes on the market, as I have found nearly as many different opinions on this subject as there are different sorts available. It is as important to varnish a model as it is to prime it, protecting with the varnish all that hard work in painting, lining and lettering.

There are basically three different types – matt, eggshell and gloss. In my opinion, gloss varnish should have no part in finishing a small-scale model, as it looks totally wrong on anything smaller than ¼in scale. This is not to say we shouldn't use it, however, because it is particularly tough, and will protect paint very well. No, we use it as an 'undercoat' varnish, for getting transfers to stick, and then adding the final varnish over the top. If this sounds as though the whole paint finish is going to be about 1mm thick, rest assured, all four coats of paint and varnish probably will not be thicker than approximately 0.001in.

Varnishes can be applied by brush, airbrush or spray can, but obviously the airbrush is the best thing to use. All the paint manufacturers mentioned earlier provide varnishes to go with their paints, of which I find very useful, Precision's Extra Pale Matt, for an absolutely dead matt finish,

and the Floquil range. Floquil Flat Finish is a superb eggshell finish which I use on most of my models.

Varnishes should be applied in the same way as we have been applying paint. Practice until you are happy with the finish before applying it to your model. It will be very tempting to rush at this stage, but resist the temptation. It would be silly to spoil the model at this stage.

To sum up, each stage of finishing a model should not be rushed, as impatience can only spoil your hard work. If you follow the steps I have outlined, there should be no reason why all those kits you have halfbuilt or even built, should not be painted.

CHAPTER 22
STARTING FROM SCRATCH

There are some, and until recently I was one of them, who are of the opinion that if you have a workshop full of sophisticated equipment, it makes it easier to produce scratchbuilt models, which is to an extent true. What is overlooked, however, is that, if you do have the equipment, the work produced must therefore be that much better and, when running at that level, mistakes are all too easy to make and the job has to be done again. Second rate is just not acceptable, so in real terms it's harder.

At the heart of any workshop is a lathe. This Myford has performed stirling work.

A standard milling machine which can also be set-up as a riveting tool.

The most sophisticated piece of equipment in the workshop is a Pantograph Miller.

A separate book would be required to cover scratchbuilding, but a book well worth a read is entitled *A Guide to Locomotive Building from Prototype to Small Scale Models*, priced £4.95, published by The Oakwood Press, 10 Swindon Road, Cricklade, Swindon SN6 6BG. Vic Green, probably the best model maker in this country, using his excellent machinery and equipment, shows how he would go about producing a pair of coupling rods for a 4mm scale LNWR 0–4–2 crane tank engine. Vic's workshop is, to say the least, fairly extensive – major pieces of equipment include 5in lathe, drilling machine, bandsaw, milling machine, guillotine and a pantograph milling machine. It is the latter that most of the bulkier components were made on.

To start, general arrangement drawings, weight diagrams and good clear photos are required. Four times masters needed to be

As a pair of coupling rods are required for the loco, two pieces of nickel silver are soldered together.

Measuring off from a four times up drawing gives us the dimensions for a master for the Pantograph Miller.

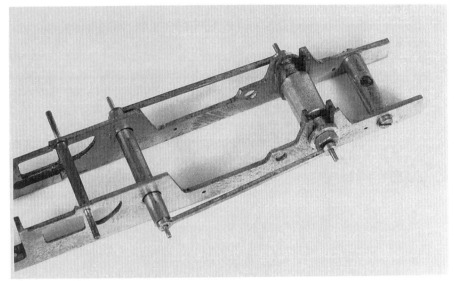

Frames and coupling rods show the crispness of the machined parts.

The Pantograph Miller was then used for the footplate. Note the inset halfway down.

These four photos (see p139) show the highest standard of workmanship that Vic Green achieves with his models. This BR 9F 2–10–0 was built to 7mm scale and took several months' full-time work. He even produces his own wheels – the ultimate in model railways.

produced so the relevant photos and paperwork needed to be of the same order. The component being made, in this case the coupling rod, is marked out onto a piece of brass sheet. The journals are carefully measured and accordingly marked onto the piece of brass. Once the component has been marked out, then a double check of all the measurements is made against the marked out piece; check it twice, do the job once.

Now using a jeweller's saw and a V-plate, the four times master is carefully cut out; not cutting up to the line, but a little way from it. The next operation is to file carefully the remaining excess metal back to the marked line. Note that both the saw and file are used at 90° to the workpiece with downward strokes. When all is complete, the final product is once again checked and put against the original drawing. The master is now mounted on the plate at the top of the pantograph miller and a suitable piece of ⅛in nickel silver is mounted on the lower machine bed. The ⅛in nickel silver has been mounted onto a scrap piece of metal with double-sided tape to ensure that the cutter doesn't damage the machine bed.

Now, carefully holding the cutting head and follower pin against the master, the cutter is gently lowered onto the workpiece and the coupling rods carefully profiled out. Once you have the master, any number of scale components can be produced and, of course, they will all be exactly the same.

This operation certainly took a considerable length of time to produce two coupling rods, but the resulting components speak for themselves – very crisp and solid, unlike the etched equivalents that have soft edges and are thin.

A further situation where this type of equipment came into its own was in producing the footplate, which has a kink in it halfway down where it gets narrower or wider depending on your point of view. The rebate, at the edge of the footplate, of course, is also extended all the way down the side, and, as can be seen, the machine produces it exactly. As a matter of interest, this was the third attempt at producing this item, as small errors in the machining are usually irretrievable. This gives you some idea as to the amount of detail that can be achieved by the professional model maker.

APPENDIX A
UK MANUFACTURERS AND SUPPLIERS

ASP
Argus House
Boundary Way
Hemel Hempstead
Herts, HP2 7ST

Carr's Modelling Products
Unit 5 Centre 88
Elm Grove
London SW19 4HE

Crownline Models
8 Rame Terrace
Rame Cross
Nr Penryn
Cornwall, TR10 9DZ

Fox Transfers
150 Upper New Walk
Leicester, LE1 7QA

Frattons
126 West Street
Fareham
Hants

Hornby Railways
Westwood
Margate
Kent, CT9 4JX

Howes
9–10 Broad Street
Oxford, OX1 3AJ

Lima Model Railways
Riko International
Hemel Hempstead
Herts, HP1 3AD

Litesold
97–99 Gloucester Road
Croydon, CRO 2DN

Model Images
56 Station Road
Letchworth
Herts, SG6 3BE

Model Masters
50a Clifton Road
Weston-super-Mare
Avon, BS23 1BW

Morris and Ingram (London) Ltd
156 Stanley Green Road
Poole
Dorset, BH15 3BE

Orton Models Peterborough
36 Hereward Cross
Peterborough

Orynx
Portman Road
Reading
Berks, RG3 1NE

Peco
Beer, Seaton
Devon, EX12 3NA

Railway Lines
2 London Road
Aston Clinton
Bucks HP22 5HQ

Replica Railways
Station Yard
Station Road
Lambourn
Berks, RG16 7PH

RJH Model Railways
Unit 19, Wessex Trade Centre
Ringwood Road
Dorset, BH12 3PF

Scale Link Co.
54 Church Street
Twickenham
London TW1 3NR

W & H (Models) Ltd
14 Cavendish Street
London, W1

Victors
166 Pentonville Road
Islington
London N1 9JL

APPENDIX B
GLOSSARY

Abutment lateral support at the end of an arch or bridge.

Adhesion contact between wheel and rail.

Ballast material placed between sleepers.

Banking assisting a train ascending a gradient by attaching one or more locos at the rear.

Bay Platform short terminal platform let into a longer one.

Bogie short wheelbase truck with four or six wheels which can pivot at the centre at which it is attached to the underframe of a loco vehicle.

Cab Control operating one or more model trains singly or simultaneously.

Cant amount by which one rail of a curved track is raised above the other.

Catenary supporting cable for conductive wire of an overhead electrification system.

Coupling device for connecting vehicles together.

Diagram display of track work and signals controlled by a signalbox.

Distant Signal signal warning approaching trains of the state of stop signals ahead.

End-to-End layout with a terminal at either end.

Fiddle Yard set of sidings where trains are terminated and stored.

Fishplates metal or plastic (insulated) plates for joining rail lengths together.

Flange inside projecting edge of a wheel.

Freelance a model not directly based on an actual prototype.

Gauge distance between rails of a track.

Gradient/Grade slope or inclination to the horizontal.

Halt stopping place without station facilities for local lines.

Headshunt road running parallel with the main line for shunting.

Home Signal semaphore stop signal.

Hump Yard marshalling yard with artificial mound for the purpose of gravity wagon sorting.

Inspection Saloon Chief Medical Engineer's private coach.

Island Platform platform with tracks on both sides.

Key wedge of wood or steel holding rail in the chair bolted to the sleeper in position at the correct gauge.

Level Crossing where two railways or a road and railway cross at the same level.

Light Engine locomotive without a train.

Limit of Shunt board marking the limit of the shunt area.

Load Gauge the limiting height and width of rolling stock and loads to ensure adequate lineside clearance.

Loop continuous circular connection between up and down lines.

Marshalling Yard place where wagons are sorted and assembled into trains.

Motor Bogie bogie with driving wheels or motorised axles.

Multiple Track section of track with more than one up and one down line.

Multiple Unit a 'set' of coaches internally powered by diesel or electric motors, operated by one driver.

Narrow Gauge railway track of less than the standard gauge of 4ft 8½in.

Packing maintaining the correct sleeper level by adjusting the ballast.

Pantagraph link between overhead catenary system and the train or loco.

Permanent Way track bed and tracks in position.

Pilot extra loco coupled to the front end of the train loco to give extra power over steep gradients.

Platelayer track maintenance man.

Point place at which trains can be directed onto another line.

Pullman Car railway carriage providing high standard of comfort and service.

Rail Car self-propelled passenger-carrying vehicle.

Rolling-Stock carriages and wagons.

Scenic Break a block in a layout to separate differing scenic backgrounds.

Semaphore type of signal with a pivoted arm which can be raised or lowered.

Set Back reversal of a train into a siding.

Shunt to move vehicles onto a minor track, to marshal vehicles into a particular order.

Shuttle regular return service over a short route.

Siding line used for temporary accommodation of vehicles.

Six-Footway area between parallel tracks.

Sleeper beam for holding rails to correct gauge.

Solebar main frame part of wagon underframe.

Standard Gauge 4ft 8½in. between rails.

Starter Signal signal giving authority to a train to proceed.

Tail Lamp lamp located at the rear of the last vehicle.

Tank Locomotive loco which carries coal and water supplies on its own main frames.

Tank Wagon freight vehicle built to carry liquid or gas in a tank-like container.

Tender Locomotive loco which carries its coal supplies in a separate permanently-coupled vehicle called a tender.

Terminal end of the line or departure point, including station, switches, buildings and other equipment.

Turntable a rotating mechanism which turns locos around.

Underbridge underline bridge carrying train over road, river etc.

Underframe framework under the body of a carriage.